333 Idioms + Phrases

For Business Including 3 Examples For Each

Liam Lusk & Scott Worden

333 Idioms + Phrases

For Business Including 3 Examples For Each

Artam Publishing

Liam Lusk & Scott Worden

Introduction

Understanding which idiom or phrase to use in a particular business situation isn't easy. Some are more suitable than others depending on location. This is why the authors Liam Lusk (British) and Scott Worden (American) decided together to write this book.

333 Idioms and Phrases for Business was written to help English learners to easily understand and use commonly spoken business expressions in everyday life. Not only can they be used in everyday life, but they can also be used both in the United Kingdom and the United States.

The authors have defined each idiom while giving the reader three examples of how to use them.

Here is an example:

In the loop

Meaning:

If you're **in the loop**, you are fully informed about what is happening in a certain area or activity.

Examples of use:
1. Please keep me **in the loop**. I don't want to be the last one to know what's happening.
2. Kelly is always **in the loop** at work. She

communicates with her boss well and knows what is expected of her every day.

3. Since I live so far away from my family, I'm never **in the loop** with what's going on with my brothers and sisters.

Aa

Above board

Meaning:
If something is done '**above board**', then it is carried out in a legal and proper manner.

Examples of use:
1. We need to make sure that everything is **above board** before we continue. We don't want to be sued for it later.
2. I'm not sure that this is really **above board**. We need to think more about this before we get into legal trouble.
3. After looking through this contract, I'm not so sure that it is **above board**. It doesn't seem very ethical.

Across the board

Meaning:
If something applies to everyone, it is '**across the board**'.

Examples of use:
1. Our company increased salaries **across the board** last year. Everyone was happy about it.
2. I have decided to change the conditions **across the board** for vacation entitlement. All employees are included.

3. We need to consider this **across the board**. How will it affect our budget?

Against the clock

Meaning:
If you do something **against the clock**, you are rushed and have very little time to do it in.

Examples of use:
1. We are going **against the clock** on this project, so we will need to work overtime tonight.
2. The stress is getting too much; we are always working **against the clock** in every deal.
3. The rescue workers were working **against the clock** to find more survivors.

Ahead of the pack

Meaning:
When you are **ahead of the pack**, you have made more progress than your rivals.

Examples of use:
1. When it comes to technology, they are definitely **ahead of the pack**, while everyone strives to be like them.
2. Over the last five years we have fallen behind. We need to get **ahead of the pack** again.
3. As a premier league player, he is **ahead of the**

pack when it comes to talent.

Ahead of time

Meaning:
If something happens **ahead of time**, it is completed early or before a set time.

Examples of use:
1. We are showing good progress with the new product line. We are **ahead of time**.
2. What has gone wrong? You told me your team was **ahead of time** last week.
3. We should buy **ahead of time** if we want to avoid the crowd.

All your eggs in one basket

Meaning:
If you put **all your eggs in one basket**, you risk everything at once, instead of trying to spread the risk. (This can often be used as a negative imperative- 'Don't put **all your eggs in one basket**'. **'Have your eggs in one basket'** is also used.)

Examples of use:
1. They went bankrupt because they put **all their eggs in one basket**. When you put all your money into one area, you can lose it all.
2. If we agree with this contract, we are putting **all**

our eggs in one basket, which is too risky.
3. When investing money it is common sense not to put **all your eggs in one basket**. You need to invest your money in different areas.

Around the clock

Meaning:
If something is open **around the clock**, it is open 24 hours a day.

Examples of use:
1. If we want to stay in business, we need to consider being open **around the clock**.
2. The restaurant chain became successful because they are open **around the clock**.
3. It's not easy to find staff for a store that is open **around the clock**.

At cross purposes

Meaning
If people are **at cross purposes**, they misunderstand each other or have different or opposing objectives.

Examples of use:
1. We shouldn't put John and Sharon on the same team. They are always **at cross purposes**.
2. Instead of being **at cross purposes,** we need to find a way to work together, otherwise we won't

achieve our goal.

3. The stress of being **at cross purposes** with my boss all the time is too much. I'm going to give in my notice.

Bb

Back burner

Meaning:
If an issue is on the **back burner**, it has been given low priority.

Examples of use:
1. We have more important tasks to deal with, so let's put this on the **back burner**.
2. Why don't we put this on the **back burner** until next month? Then we will have more time to concentrate on it.
3. We don't have the resources at the moment, so we should put it on the **back burner** for the moment.

Back to square one

Meaning:
If you go **back to square one**, you have to start from the beginning again.

Examples of use:
1. The production process went wrong somewhere, so we need to go **back to square one**.
2. We have obviously gone wrong in the initial set-up. Let's go **back to square one** and get it done right.
3. If we go **back to square one,** we will have lost six months of hard work.

Back to the drawing board

Meaning:
If you need to go **back to the drawing board**, you have to go back to the beginning and start something again.

Examples of use:
1. This isn't good enough to use. We need to go **back to the drawing board** and try again.
2. They went **back to the drawing board** after the prototype failed.
3. I know your team has worked very hard on this, but we can't offer this to the client. You need to go **back to the drawing board** and do it all over again.

Ball is in your court

Meaning:
When the **ball is in your court**, it is up to you to make the next decision or take the next step.

Examples of use:
1. We've given them our best offer, so the **ball is in their court** now.
2. I've told him to apologize if he wants it back. The **ball's in his court** now.
3. We made a good offer for the house and now the **ball is in their court**.

Ballpark figure

Meaning:
A **ballpark figure** is an acceptable, roughly accurate approximation.

Examples of use:
1. Can't you at least give us a **ballpark figure** so we have some idea of the cost?
2. We don't know the population exactly but a **ball park figure** would be about 1.5 million.
3. I wouldn't depend on their **ballpark figure** there are always hidden costs that come up later.

Beck and call

Meaning:
Someone who does everything for you without question, no matter when you ask is at your **beck and call**.

Examples of use:
1. You don't to need to be at her **beck and call** for 24 hours.
2. I heard that John quit his job because he was fed up with being at their **beck and call**.
3. We're not at their **beck and call** and they need to understand that. We are not their slaves.

Below par

Meaning:
If something isn't up to standard, or when someone isn't feeling or doing very well, they are **below par**.

Examples of use:
1. I'm really feeling **below par** today. I didn't sleep much.
2. Your team's performance has been **below par** recently. Is there a problem I should know about?
3. Their service has been **below par** this last month. Perhaps we should reconsider our contract with them.

Big bucks

Meaning:
If someone is making **big bucks**, they are making a large amount of money.

Examples of use:
1. This is a great opportunity to make some **big bucks**.
2. I don't understand why he earns the **big bucks** when his work is so bad.
3. If we do this right, we could start making the **big bucks**.

Big cheese

Meaning:
The **big cheese** is an important or powerful person in a group or organization.

Examples of use:
1. I'm fed up with him thinking he's the **big cheese** around here. He's not the C.E.O.
2. One day I will be the **big cheese** in this company, so she better watch out.
3. Did you know that his father is the **big cheese** in this industry? He has a lot of power and cash flow.

Big picture

Meaning:
The **big picture** of something is the complete perspective or objective of something.

Examples of use:
1. The sales director gave us the **big picture** earlier today. Now I understand.
2. We need to understand the **big picture** before we can go any further with this.
3. I don't really understand the **big picture** here. Can you explain it again for me?

Blackball

Meaning:
To **blackball** someone is to exclude/ostracize them socially, to reject them.

1. I heard that he was **blackballed** from the industry after they went bankrupt. No one can trust him because his reputation was ruined.
2. If you're not careful, they could **blackball** you from the club.
3. I don't understand why they tried to **blackball** me, but they're going to answer for it.

Blow the whistle

Meaning:
If you **blow the whistle**, you report the wrong doing of a person, group or organization to the authorities.

Examples of use:
1. I know that my company isn't meeting regulations, but if I **blow the whistle** I could lose my job.
2. After **blowing the whistle** on an unethical company, he became a celebrity.
3. You need to **blow the whistle** because too many people are getting hurt.

Bottom line

Meaning:
The **bottom line** is net income, and is used idiomatically to mean the conclusion.

Examples of use:
1. We failed to make the **bottom line** again this month. I think we need to change our sales strategy.
2. The **bottom line** is that we need to cut our staff back by making redundancies.
3. They can't afford to pay us this month. That's the **bottom line**.

Bounce ideas

Meaning:
If you **bounce ideas** off someone, you share your ideas with them to find out if they think they would work.

Examples of work:
1. Let's **bounce** some **ideas** around and see if we come up with a solution.
2. If we **bounce ideas** off each other, I'm sure we can think of something amazing.
3. They work really well together because they can **bounce ideas** off each other.

Break even

Meaning:
If you **break even**, you don't make any money, but you don't lose any either.

Examples of use:
1. You're lucky if you **break even** in the first year of business. You're almost expected to lose money.
2. Congratulations everyone! We have finally **broken even**, so now we can move forward with confidence.
3. The economy has hit us hard this year, so I don't think we're going to **break even** with sales.

Bring to the table

Meaning:
When you **bring something to the table**, you make a contribution or an offer in a discussion or negotiation.

Example of use:
1. Is this all we have to **bring to the table**? We need to have something better than this weak offer.
2. They won't expect us to **bring** anything **to the table**. This is going to be easy.
3. Now you know what we need. What have you **brought to the table**?

Bull market

Meaning:
When investors are optimistic and there are expectations that good financial results will continue, it is a **bull market**.

Examples of use:
1. Now is the time to act with this **bull market**. We have potential to make a lot of money.
2. We can't go wrong in this **bull market**. Let's start investing now.
3. Our investment is going to give us a tidy return in this **bull market**.

Burn the candle at both ends

Meaning:
If you **burn the candle at both ends**, you work very hard and stay up very late at night.

Examples of use:
1. No wonder John is so ill. He's been **burning the candle at both ends**.
2. If you continue to **burn the candle at both ends**, you'll wear yourself out.
3. I don't get paid enough to **burn the candle at both ends**.

Cc

Call the shots

Meaning:
If you **call the shots**, you are in charge and tell people what to do.

Examples of use:
1. How long has John been **calling the shots** around here? I thought someone else was in charge of everything.
2. I just wanted to let you all know that I will be **calling the shots** around here from now on. If you need something, contact me first.
3. Julie thinks she **calls the shots** around here, but everyone knows that it's really Mary who does.

Can't hack (something)

Meaning:
This means you are unable to perform an act, duty, job etc.

Examples of use:
1. I don't think James **can hack** his new responsibilities. We need to tell someone.
2. I feel it is time for me to resign. I **can't hack** all this new technology.
3. We made a mistake allowing that team to take the contract. They **can't hack** it!

Can't see the forest for its trees

Meaning:
If someone **can't see the forest for its trees**, they are too focused on specific details to see the bigger picture.

Examples of use:
1. I got so involved in the wording of the contract, that I **couldn't see the forest for the trees**; I didn't realize that the contract would never work.
2. Chris **can't see the forest for the trees.** He always argues about the petty cash but fails to consider the budget.
3. After years of researching the same topic, it's understandable that you **can't see the forest for the trees**.

Card up your sleeve

Meaning:
If you have a **card up your sleeve**, you have a surprise plan or idea that you are holding back until the time is right.

Examples of use:
1. We need a **card up our sleeve** before we start negotiating with this company. Otherwise they will destroy us.

2. I have a **card up my sleeve** to make this deal more attractive.
3. We still have a **card up our sleeve**; we have the new technology that they need.

Carrot and stick

Meaning:
If someone offers a **carrot and stick**, they offer an incentive to do something combined with the threat of punishment.

Examples of use:
1. They're proposed deal is great; it's all **carrot and no stick**.
2. In the latest round of talks we have seen both the **carrot and the stick** of the situation.
3. Sometimes I need to use the **carrot and stick** method with my employees.

Carry the can

Meaning:
When you **carry the can**, you take the blame for something, even though you didn't do it or are only partly at fault.

Examples of use:
1. Whenever Roger does something wrong we have to **carry the can**. It isn't fair. Roger should be

responsible for his mistakes.

2. John had to **carry the can** for his department manager again. He said he's had enough and will not take the blame for him anymore.

3. As usual, I was left to **carry the can** after you messed up.

Case by case

Meaning:
When we things are done **case by case**, each situation or issue is handled separately on its own merits and demerits.

Examples of use:
1. We need to look at every complaint **case by case**, because they require different solutions.

2. Every suggestion needs to be considered carefully on a **case by case** basis.

3. I can't give you a general answer on your queries. We need to look at each one **case by case**.

Case in point

Meaning:
An instance when something has just occurred that was previously discussed. For instance, a person may have told another that something always happens. Later that day, they see it happening, and the informer might say, **'case in point'**.

Examples of use:
1. Elizabeth is proving too unpredictable and yesterday is a good **case in point**.
2. Their turn around in productivity is amazing and last month was a **case in point**.
3. Our safety measures need to be improved. John Smith's accident last week is a **case in point**.

Cash in your chips

Meaning:
When you **cash in your chips**, you sell something to get what profit you can, because you think its value is going to fall. It can also mean 'to die'.

Examples of use:
1. We should **cash in our chips**, so we can pay them off.
2. Profits were low, so Justine **cashed in her chips**.
3. I would suggest that we **cash in our chips** now before we lose any more money.

Catch-22

Meaning:
Catch-22 is a situation where conflicting rules make the desired outcome impossible. It comes from a novel by the American author Joseph Heller, in which pilots would not have to fly missions if they

were mentally ill. But not wanting to fly dangerous missions was held to be proof of sanity, so they had to fly anyway.

Examples of use:
1. This has put us in a real **catch-22**. If we agree or disagree either side suffers.
2. You've got me in a real **catch-22** here with Peter. No matter which decision I choose, I might have a problem.
3. I can't get a job without an address and I can't get an address without a job. It's a **catch-22**.

Change horses in midstream

Meaning:
When people **change horses in midstream**, they change plans or leaders when they are in the middle of something, even though it may be very risky to do so.

Examples of use:
1. The final draft is almost complete. It's too late to change the legal team. You can't **change horses in midstream**.
2. Our factory has already started production. We can't **change horses in midstream**. It would be financial suicide.
3. I know it was risky, but by **changing horses in midstream** I won the contract.

Change tack

Meaning:
If you change tack, you use a different method for dealing with something.

Examples of use:
1. I wish Roger would stop **changing tack** all the time. It's really confusing.
2. Our negotiation method isn't working. We need to **change tack** quickly before we lose this deal.
3. Maybe we need to consider **changing tack** if we want to succeed with this.

Change your tune

Meaning:
If someone changes their ideas or the way they talk about them, they **change their tune**.

Examples of use:
1. You've **changed your tune** since we last talked. What changed your mind?
2. They suddenly **changed their tune** and agreed with my opinion when they found out I owned the company.
3. You should think about **changing your tune** if you want to get on with people around here.

Chase rainbows

Meaning:
If someone is **chasing a rainbow**, they try to do something that they will never achieve.

Examples of use:
1. You need to stop **chasing rainbows** and get a real job. Your business ideas never work.
2. Everybody said John was **chasing rainbows** until he proved them wrong and became C.E.O.
3. One of the problems with being an entrepreneur is that everyone tells you that you're **chasing rainbows** and not being realistic.

Chase your tail

Meaning:
If you are **chasing your tail**, you are very busy but not being very productive.

Examples of use:
1. We've been working on this project for weeks, but now we're just **chasing our tails**.
2. I've had enough of your opinion. You always **chase your tail** but don't get enough work done.
3. I feel like even with all our hard work we have just been **chasing our tails**.

Chew the cud

Meaning:
If you **chew the cud**, you think carefully about something.

Examples of use:
1. John has been **chewing the cud** all morning about what Jill said yesterday.
2. I don't understand what there is to **chew the cud** about. It's simple enough, so we don't need to go over it any more.
3. You've **chewed the cud** enough about this. What is your decision?

Child's play

Meaning:
We use the phrase **child's play** when we want to say that something is very easy and simple.

Examples of use:
1. I can't understand why Jane can't get these reports correct. They're **child's play**.
2. Getting this deal is going to be **child's play**, so don't worry.
3. We were foolish to think that the negotiation was going to be **child's play**. It's been a lot harder than we expected.

Circling the drain

Meaning:
If something is **circling the drain**, a project or plan or campaign is on the brink of failure.

Examples of use:
1. This project has been **circling the drain** for a while now. We should stop now before it gets worse.
2. The problem with David's plan is that it has been **circling the drain** since the beginning and I don't want to see it fall apart.
3. This company has been **circling the drain** for too long now. We need to get out before it goes out of business.

Come up trumps

Meaning:
When someone is said to have **'come up trumps'**, they have completed an activity successfully or produced a good result.

Examples of use:
1. I really didn't think we would get that deal. We've **come up trumps**.
2. It doesn't matter what James does. He always **comes up trumps** in everything and is always successful.
3. It would be great if we could **come up trumps** just once in a while instead of struggling all of the time.

Comes with the territory

Meaning:
If something **comes with the territory**, especially when undesirable, it is automatically included with something else, like a job or responsibility sometimes, 'Goes with the territory' is also used.

Examples of use:
1. Stress **comes with territory** in this job. You'll learn to accept that.
2. When you work in customer service, rude people **come with the territory**.
3. I heard that hard work **came with the territory**, but 16-hour days are ridiculous.

Comfort zone

Meaning:
If you are in a place where you feel comfortable, where you can avoid the worries of the world you are in your **comfort zone**.

Examples of use:
1. In my last job I was way out of my **comfort zone**. However, this company is great.
2. I know you like your position, but you should come out of your **comfort zone** and try something challenging.

3. You told me that this was in your **comfort zone**, Jeff. What went wrong?

Connect the dots

Meaning:
If you **connect the dots**, you understand the connections and relationships.

Examples of use:
1. Once we **connect the dots** on this, it will be simple.
2. **Connecting the dots** on this deal won't be easy. I think we need more help.
3. It's taken a long time to **connect the dots** on this one, but we should feel proud that we're on the right track now.

Cook the books

Meaning:
If people **cook the books**, they keep false accounts to make money illegally or to avoid paying taxes.

Examples of use:
1. It looks like they have been **cooking the books** for years. How did they not get caught earlier?
2. George, I hope that you aren't suggesting we **cook the books** because that's illegal.
3. When did they first start **cooking the books**? I

never realized they never paid enough taxes.

Corner a market

Meaning:
If a business is dominant in an area and unlikely to be challenged by other companies, it has **cornered the market**.

Examples of use:
1. They've **cornered the market** for over a decade, so they're going to be hard to beat.
2. If we plan this correctly, we can **corner the market** with this product and dominate the competition.
3. Let's make a goal to **corner the market** within the next five years and be successful in this business area.

Cover all the bases

Meaning:
If you are **covering all the bases**, you deal with all aspects of a situation or issue, or anticipate all possibilities. (You can also use '**Cover all bases'**)

Examples of use:
1. We need to make sure that we have **covered all our bases** on this one. We don't know what bad things could possibly happen, so we should be

prepared.
2. This is really good you've **covered all the bases**. Now we are clear on all aspects of the issues.
3. Make sure you **cover all bases** when you plan the promotion, so that everyone understands where you're coming from.

Cream of the crop

Meaning:
The cream of the crop is when something/someone is the best there is.

Examples of use:
1. This particular motorcycle is the cream of the crop. No other motorcycle comes close to the power and ingenuity.
2. These groups of designers are very talented. They are the **cream of the crop**.
3. If we want our employees to be the **cream of the crop**, we need to give them more benefits.

Cream rises to the top

Meaning:
This means that a good person or idea cannot go unnoticed for long, just as cream poured in coffee or tea eventually **rises to the top**.

Examples of use:

1. You didn't get the promotion today, but you will don't worry **cream** always **rises to the top**.
2. They didn't accept our idea today, but **cream** always **rises to the top** don't worry.
3. I told you that **cream** always **rises to the top**. Now enjoy your promotion.

Cross swords

Meaning:
When people cross swords, they argue or dispute.

Examples of use:
1. I don't understand why we continue to do business with them. We are always **crossing swords** with them.
2. We don't always agree. In fact, I've **crossed swords** with her several times at monthly meetings.
3. I wish we could just agree once. We are always **crossing swords** when we meet.

Crunch time

Meaning:
When making an important decision that will have a considerable effect on their future, it is **crunch time**.

Examples of use:
1. Today is **crunch time**, so we will need to work overtime I'm afraid.

2. It is **crunch time** everybody, so let's hope we did the job right.
3. I know it is **crunch time**, but I feel that we could improve this if we had a bit more time.

Curve ball

Meaning:
(USA) If something is a **curve ball**, it is deceptive.

Examples of use:
1. I thought I understood the math concept, but then the teacher threw me a **curveball** and then I was confused again.
2. The deal would have gone through, but the client through me a **curveball** by asking for a larger contract at the last minute.
3. Don't throw me any **curveballs**. Just give me an honest answer.

Cut and run

Meaning:
If people **cut and run**, they take what they can get and leave before they lose everything.

Examples of use:
1. The business is losing money fast. I'm going to **cut and run** before I go completely bankrupt.

2. Enron employees probably hoped they would have **cut and run** before the company went completely under.
3. Since my poker hands are pretty bad tonight, I'm going to **cut and run** before I go home with an empty wallet.

Cut corners

Meaning:

If people try to do something as cheaply or as quickly as possible, often sacrificing quality, they are **cutting corners**.

Examples of use:
1. **Cutting corners** on constructing a building is very dangerous. If an earthquake happens, many people could die from the lack of care put into building the structure.
2. Teachers hate it when students **cut corners** when they do their homework in order to get it done as quickly as possible.
3. If the construction workers **cut corners**, it may cause the streets to have potholes within a few months.

Cut the mustard

Meaning:

(UK) If somebody or something doesn't **cut the mustard**, they fail or it fails to reach the required standard.

Examples of use:
1. Although John has only been an employee for a month, he isn't **cutting the mustard**. He is too slow and makes a lot of mistakes.
2. I really hope she can **cut the mustard**, because this company cannot afford to have another lazy employee.
3. Your typing skills don't **cut the mustard**. Once your skills improve, please apply for the position again.

Cut to the chase

Meaning:

If you **cut to the chase**, you get to the point, or the most interesting or important part of something without delay.

Examples of use:
1. Please **cut to the chase**. This is really important and I need to know now.
2. I wish the media would **cut to the chase** and not wait until the last minute to show us the important news.

3. Let me **cut to the chase** and not prolong this any longer. You're fired!

Cut your losses

Meaning:

If you **cut your losses**, you avoid losing any more money than you already have by getting out of a situation before matters worsen.

Examples of use:
1. Our business doesn't look very promising. We might as well **cut our losses** before we lose a lot more money.
2. That investment isn't panning out. We better **cut our losses** before we lose more money than we already have.
3. The stocks keep plunging every day. **Cut your losses** before you really regret it later!

Cutting edge

Meaning:

Something that is **cutting edge** is at the forefront of progress in its area.

Examples of use:

39

1. CD players used to be on the **cutting edge** of technology before MP3 players came out.
2. Many people want to be on the **cutting edge** of a new product in order to become rich.
3. Just when you think something is on the **cutting edge**, something new replaces it.

Dd

Dead duck

Meaning:

If something is a **dead duck**, it is a failure.

Examples of use:
1. You're going to be a **dead duck** if you continue to come to work late. The boss will consider firing you or giving you a written warning.
2. Even though I was a **dead duck** in business, I've succeeded in teaching.
3. Steve is a **dead duck**. He messed up the report again.

Dead in the water

Meaning:

If something is **dead in the water**, it isn't going anywhere or making any progress.

Examples of use:
1. This contract seems **dead in the water**. We've tried to negotiate for the past six months, but it isn't going anywhere.
2. They were supposed to open that hotel in downtown last year, but the deal seems to be **dead in**

the water. That building is still vacant as we speak.
3. The marriage is **dead in the water**. The families just don't seem to support their marriage.

Dead man walking

Meaning:

A **dead man walking** is someone who is in great trouble and will certainly get punished, lose their job or position, etc. soon.

Examples of use:
1. Johnny is a **dead man walking**. He lied to his parents about his grades. Once they find out, he'll be grounded for at least a month.
2. George sexually harassed his secretary. He's a **dead man walking**. I'm sure he'll be fired within the next few days.
3. She seems like a **dead man walking**. She's lazy and does nothing but gossip at work.

Dead men's shoes

Meaning:

If promotion or success requires replacing somebody, then it can only be reached by **dead men's shoes**' by getting rid of them.

Examples of use:
1. If we want this company to succeed, then we have to consider the **dead men's shoes** although I hate firing people.
2. We need to know who the **dead men's shoes** are if we want to get our company recognized in the industry.
3. Whose **dead men's shoes** are they? They're bringing the organization down.

Devil is in the detail

Meaning:

When people say that the **devil is in the detail**, they mean that small things in plans and schemes that are often overlooked can cause serious problems later on.

Examples of use:
1. The **devil is in the detail** of that plan. Although it sounds good, it will hurt us in the long run.
2. If we aren't careful, the **devil might be in the detail**. We don't want this scheme to come back to haunt us in the future.
3. I really hope the **devil is not in the detail**. I want these plans to turn out well.

Dip your toes in the water

Meaning:

If you **dip your toes in the water**, you try
something tentatively, because you are not sure
whether it will work or not.

Examples of use:
1. Before we go along with the plan, let's **dip our toes in the water** and see if it works.
2. I don't like blind dates, but I might as well **dip my toes in the water** and find out if I can get the man of my dreams.
3. She **dipped her toes in the water** with a cookie recipe. She wasn't sure if they would taste good, but she wanted to find out.

Dish out the dirt

Meaning:

If you **dish out the dirt** on something or someone, you make unpleasant or shocking information public.

Examples of use:
1. If you gossip about me, I will **dish out the dirt** about your past and embarrass you.
2. The tabloids love to **dish out the dirt** on certain celebrities to make a lot of money.
3. Anyone who **dishes out the dirt** about someone's

private life will be fired.

Do their dirty work

Meaning:

Someone who **does someone's dirty work**, carries out the unpleasant jobs that the first person doesn't want to do. Someone who seems to enjoy doing this is sometimes known as a 'henchman'.

Examples of use:
1. Brad didn't want to clean out the office, so Chris **did his dirty work** voluntarily, because he respects his boss.
2. Why do I always have to **do your dirty work**? You need to take care of your responsibilities.
3. Weak bosses **do their employees dirty work**, because they get tired of nagging them all of the time.

Dodge the bullet

Meaning:

If someone has **dodged a bullet**, they have successfully avoided a very serious problem.

Examples of use:

1. Stacy **dodged a bullet** by getting to class just as the bell rang.
2. In business, you have to make important decisions and **dodge a lot of bullets** to keep your company afloat.
3. That company's stock just went down 20 points. We **dodged a bullet** by not investing in it last year.

Dog eat dog

Meaning:

In a **dog eat dog** world, there is intense competition and rivalry, where everybody thinks only of himself or herself.

Examples of use:
1. Marketing is a great representation of a **dog eat dog** world. No one cares about the other. They all just want to succeed, even if it includes destroying their opposition.
2. It's a **dog eat dog** world in sports. No one will feel sorry for you if you lose.
3. Can you handle a **dog eat dog** environment with a bunch of arrogant and competitive employees? If so, I'll hire you.

Don't bite the hand that feeds

Meaning:

When someone says this to you, they are trying to tell you not to act against those on whom you depend on.

Examples of use:
1. **Don't bite the hand that feeds** you, Kim. Your mom takes care of you. Respect her.
2. John has a tendency to **bite the hand that feeds** him. His co-workers always help him when he has too much work, but he talks behind their backs.
3. She shouldn't **bite the hand that feeds** her. She will need those people in the future.

Don't give up your day job

Meaning:

This idiom is used as a way of telling someone that they do something badly.

Examples of use:
1. After listening to you sing, I only have one thing to say. **Don't give up your day job**!
2. **Don't give up your day job**. You're not good enough to be a professional basketball player.
3. You said you're a good dancer, but actually I think you shouldn't **give up your day job**. You're not as good as you think you are.

Don't sweat the small stuff

Meaning:

(USA) This is used to tell people not to worry about trivial or unimportant issues.

Examples of use:
1. John, **don't sweat the small stuff**. It's not that big of a deal. We can get a new mouse for the computer tomorrow.
2. Who cares if your friend forgot to call you for your birthday. Maybe she was really busy. **Don't sweat the small stuff**.
3. The internet is usually good. It's only been slow for one hour. **Don't sweat the small stuff**.

Donkey work

Meaning:
Donkey work is any hard, boring work or task.

Examples of use:
1. Doing paperwork all day for eight hours is nothing but **donkey work**. It makes me want to quit my job.
2. Why are you doing all that **donkey work**? You can get a job that pays you more and gives you less stress.
3. I'm tired of doing **donkey work**. I'm not

appreciated for my work and I get paid pennies.

Dot all the i's and cross all the t's

Meaning:

If you **dot all the I's and cross all the T's**, you do something very carefully and thoroughly.

Examples of use:
1. I better **dot all the I's and cross all the T's** before I choose this position.
2. Before you consider marrying that person, make sure that you **dot all the I's and cross all the T's**.
3. She wants to buy a nice house, but she is **dotting all the I's and crossing all the T's** before she makes her decision on which one to buy.

Down the drain

Meaning:

If something **goes down the drain,** especially money or work, it is wasted or produces no results.

Examples of use:
1. I spent $100 on lottery tickets and didn't win. That was money **down the drain**.
2. Your chances of landing that position will **go**

down the drain if you're late for the interview.
3. He was boring on the first date. His chances of a second date might have just **gone down the drain**.

Drag your feet

Meaning:

If someone is **dragging their feet**, they are taking too long to do or finish something, usually because they don't want to do it.

Examples of use:
1. Quit **dragging your feet**. Go on that blind date. He might be a nice guy!
2. The young girl was **dragging her feet** when her mom told her to wash the dishes. She really wanted to hang out with her friends and do the dishes later.
3. Ben **dragged his feet** when he was told to write a 15-page report about the periodic table and how it originated. He definitely wasn't motivated to do it.

Draw a blank

Meaning:

If you try to find something out and **draw a blank**, you don't get any useful information.

Examples of use:
1. The officer tried to ask neighbors if they had seen the robber, but no one had seen him. They **drew a blank**.
2. The doctors wanted to find out what happened to Cathy during her car accident, but she wasn't sure what happened. She might have **drawn a blank** due to the impact of her accident.
3. Whenever I try to ask middle school students about their lives, I **draw blanks**. They never seem to want to tell me about what happens to them at home.

Drive home

Meaning:

The idiomatic expression '**drive home**' means 'reinforce' as in 'The company offered unlimited technical support as a way to drive home the message that customer satisfaction was its highest priority.'

Examples of use:
1. In order to get his boss to understand the situation, he **drove home** the point that in order to increase sales, the company had to lower their costs.
2. The students don't understand why homework is important. I need to **drive home** the point more clearly.
3. To show how much market share the company was losing to their competition, John made slides to

drive home the point.

Drop in the ocean

Meaning:

A **drop in the ocean** implies that something will have little effect because it is small and mostly insignificant.

Examples of use:
1. Millionaires that donate $100 to natural disasters is helpful, but it's a **drop in the ocean** compared to how much they could actually donate.
2. The company needed $25,000 to get out of bankruptcy. Although Tom felt his contribution was just a **drop in the ocean**, the company was very thankful for it.
3. Even though it's just a **drop in the ocean**, I would like to come over for a couple of hours to help you build your home.

Drop the ball

Meaning

If someone **drops the ball**, they are not doing their job or taking their responsibilities seriously enough and let something go wrong.

Meaning:

1. Edwin's boss asked him to order some dress shoes for him because a very important business trip was approaching. However, Edwin **dropped the ball** by ordering the wrong sized shoes.
2. I have to make sure I don't **drop the ball** when I give my presentation to the whole company. If I stutter or hesitate, it could be a huge embarrassment.
3. Jenny **dropped the ball** when she forgot to pick up her mother's clothes at the cleaners.

Dry run

Meaning:

A dry run is a full rehearsal or trial exercise of something to see how it will work before it is launched.

Meaning:
1. Let's do a **dry run** of this TV show and see how the audience reacts to it before we put it on the air.
2. Before we do our group presentation to the class, how about having a **dry run** to see if we need to change anything?
3. The 10K is next month. I better go through a **dry run** to make sure I'm ready to compete in the race.

Dry spell

Meaning:

If something or someone is having a **dry spell**, they aren't being as successful as they normally are.

Examples of use:
1. My dating life has been frustrating lately. I've been in a **dry spell** for two years.
2. Our company is in a major **dry spell**. If we don't start becoming profitable in the next six months, we may need to restructure.
3. We need to get this economy out of the **dry spell**, so we can create more jobs for the middle class.

Ducks in a row

Meaning:

(USA) If you have your **ducks in a row**, you are well-organized.

Examples of use:
1. He has his **ducks in a row**. He doesn't have any clutter on his desk.
2. Please get your **ducks in a row** or else you will lose your paperwork.
3. Christina always has her **ducks in a row**. She has her files color coordinated and in chronological order.

Ee

Eager beaver

Meaning:

A person who is extremely keen is an **eager beaver**.

Examples of use:
1. Kevin is an **eager beaver**. He always arrives to class 15 minutes early.
2. Don't be such an **eager beaver**. The boss might be thinking you are trying to win brownie points with him.
3. The teacher was surprised at how many eager **beavers** there were in class today. Many students were raising their hands to answer her questions.

Early bird catches the worm

Meaning:
The **early bird catches the worm** means that if you start something early, you stand a better chance of success.

Examples of use:
1. If you want to catch those fish, you better wake up early. The **early bird catches the worm**.
2. You know the **early bird catches the worm**. If you study now, you'll be thankful you did later.

3. Let's be the **early birds that catch the worms**. If we go shopping early, we can get out before the crowds come.

Earn a living

Meaning:

To make money

Examples of use:
1. It's almost impossible to **earn a** good **living** on minimum wage in a big city.
2. In order to have children, you must **earn a good living** in order to feed them.
3. I need to work three jobs to **earn** enough of **a living** to pay my rent each month.

Eleventh hour

Meaning:

If something happens at the **eleventh hour**, it happens right at the last minute.

Examples of use:
1. Getting that player to sign for our team almost didn't happen. It happened at the **eleventh hour** to our surprise.
2. Jane was stuck in traffic, but made it to her

meeting at the **eleventh hour** just as everyone was sitting down to begin.

3. Please don't come at the **eleventh hour**. Come early or don't come at all.

Etched in stone

Meaning:

Something, especially rules and customs, that cannot be changed at all is said to be **etched in stone**.

Examples of use:

1. Once you sign this contract, it will be **etched in stone** and you will be bound to it.

2. The teacher let the students make up the classroom rules. However, once they were **etched in stone**, they couldn't change them.

3. Marriage vows are meant to be **etched in stone**. Unfortunately, many couples don't take them seriously and get divorced.

Every trick in the book

Meaning:

If you try **every trick in the book**, you try every possible way, including dishonesty and deceit, to get what you want.

Examples of use:
1. The Giants used **every trick in the book** to win football games including stealing the other team's playbook.
2. Some politicians are so dishonest that they try **every trick in the book** to win elections.
3. Telemarketers are really sneaky. They'll use **every trick in the book** to get you to buy their products.

Explore all avenues

Meaning:

If all **avenues are being explored**, then every conceivable approach is being tried that could possibly get the desired result.

Examples of use:
1. I hope I can buy one of those houses, but I need to **explore all avenues** in order to get the one that I really want.
2. It's so hard to find the love of your life. Make sure you **explore all avenues**, so you can meet the right one.
3. There are many ways to buy the used car that we need for our family. Let's **explore all avenues** to get the best car.

Ff

Failure is the mother of success

Meaning:

Failure is often a stepping stone towards success.

Examples of use:
1. **Failure is the mother of success**. Despite many setbacks, I've learned a lot.
2. After succeeding after many difficult times, I've learned that **failure is the mother of success**.
3. Abraham Lincoln fell down many times in his life. He is a true example of **failure being the mother of success**.

Fat cat

Meaning:

A **fat cat** is a person who makes a lot of money and enjoys a privileged position in society.

Examples of use:
1. **Fat cats** enjoy the high life and don't really need to worry about health care.
2. You don't understand the struggles that the middle class has. You're just a **fat cat** that collects his salary and goes on vacation every six months.

3. Some people would say that politicians are **fat cats** who only care about making money and retiring rich.

Feather in your cap

Meaning:

A success or achievement that may help you in the future is a **feather in your cap**.

Examples of use:
1. Getting a Master's degree is one more **feather in my cap** that will help me in my teaching career.
2. If you want to get into acting, you should add a **feather to your cap** by performing on stage.
3. He got another **feather in his cap** as a writer by getting his article published in the Wall Street Journal.

Feel the pinch

Meaning:

If someone is short of money or feeling restricted in some other way, they are **feeling the pinch**.

Examples of use:
1. Lance **felt the pinch** after spending so much

money on his trip to Europe. He now has to watch what he spends carefully.

2. You don't want to **feel the pinch** after you stop working. Make sure you save enough for retirement.

3. After Steve and Carrie spent money on their children's college education, they **felt the pinch**. They decided to sell their car to ease the pain.

Feet on the ground

Meaning:

A practical and realistic person has their **feet on the ground**.

Examples of use:
1. Donna certainly has her **feet on the ground**. She has a good job, owns her own home, and lives a modest lifestyle.

2. I want to get my **feet on the ground**. I'm tired of partying, blowing money away, and then regretting it later.

3. If you want to keep your **feet on the ground**, you should set some short term goals as well as long term goals.

Fence sitter

Meaning:

Someone that tries to support both sides of an argument without committing to either is a fence sitter.

Examples of use:
1. Quit **sitting on the fence**! Tell us how you really feel about this issue.
2. I know you don't want to offend anybody, but can you please stop being a **fence sitter** and help us with this argument?
3. We can't have any **fence sitters** in this jury. We need people that are sure of themselves and not afraid to make important decisions.

Fight an uphill battle

Meaning:

When you **fight an uphill battle**, you have to struggle against very unfavorable circumstances.

Examples of use:
1. The doctor was afraid to tell the patient that he had cancer. The patient would have to prepare to **fight an uphill battle**.
2. The team lost eight games in a row. They have to **fight an uphill battle** just to get out of last place.
3. Jason's credit is really bad, so he has to **fight an uphill battle** just to get the house that he really wants.

Fight tooth and nail

Meaning:

If someone will fight tooth and nail for something, they will not stop at anything to get what they want. ('Fight tooth and claw' is an alternative.)

Examples of use:
1. I will **fight tooth and nail** to get the woman I want even if it means doing something that I wouldn't normally do to get her.
2. In well-known tourist cities, street venders will **fight tooth and nail** to get customers to buy their products.
3. The divorced couples **fought tooth and nail** over the custody of their son, but it only made the son more frustrated with both of them.

Fine tuning

Meaning:

Small adjustments to improve something or to get it working is called **fine tuning**.

Examples of use:
1. Carrie is still getting used to the job, but after a

little bit of **fine tuning**, she'll be a great employee.
2. Once our car gets some **fine tuning**, we'll be able to drive cross country.
3. We need to do a little bit of **fine tuning** to make this office look a lot more organized. It shouldn't take long.

Fire Away

Meaning:

If you want to ask someone a question and they tell you to **fire away**, they mean that you are free to ask what you want.

Examples of use:
1. Feel free to **fire away** if you're not sure about something. I would be more than happy to give you my opinion.
2. If you need some advice, just **fire away**. I can help you with any questions you have.
3. The teacher told me to **fire away** with questions if I was confused about what she had taught in class.

Fire on all cylinders

Meaning:

If something is **firing on all cylinders**, it is going as well as it can.

Examples of use:
1. The meeting is **firing on all cylinders**. We're getting a lot of feedback from everyone.
2. Once we get our employees **firing on all cylinders**, we're going to get work done on time.
3. I hope that our team **fires on all cylinders** tonight after getting all of our players back from the injury list.

First out of the gate

Meaning:

When someone is **first out of the gate**, they are the first to do something that others are trying to do.

Examples of use:
1. Kelly wanted to be **first out of the gate**, so that she could work on something else while everyone else finished their portion of the project.
2. Once a new product is launched, many people fight to be the **first out of the gate** in order to brag to their friends that they were the first one to try it.
3. No one in my family has been to Europe. I want to be **first out of the gate** to motivate everyone else to go next time.

Fit the bill

Meaning:

If something **fits the bill**, it is what is required for the task.

Examples of use:
1. This detergent **fits the bill**. It will clean my clothes properly.
2. These dress shoes should **fit the bill**. I just need them for my brother's graduation.
3. Do you think Dennis **fits the bill** or should we look for someone else?

Flogging a dead horse

Meaning:

(UK) If someone is trying to convince people to do or feel something without any hope of succeeding, they're flogging a dead horse. This is used when someone is trying to raise interest in an issue that no-one supports anymore; beating a dead horse will not make it do any more work.

Examples of use:
1. There's no use in **flogging a dead horse**. You mentioned it 10 times already.
2. Her husband kept **beating the dead horse**. She got tired of him talking about her spending habits all the time.

3. Please don't **beat the dead horse** any more. I got the point already.

Food for thought

Meaning:

If something is **food for thought**, it is worth thinking about or considering seriously.

Examples of use:
1. After listening to your presentation, I felt like it gave me a lot of **food for thought**.
2. Here's some **food for thought**. John works 10 less hours than myself and gets paid more. 3. That was an interesting **food for thought** documentary. It definitely made me think again about certain issues.

Foot the bill

Meaning:

The person who **foots the bill** pays the bill for everybody.

Examples of use:
1. Marcy **footed the bill** after the meal since she was so appreciative of working with such great employees.
2. When our family goes out to dinner, my dad **foots**

the bill because he's such a generous person.

3. Don't **foot the bill** this time. You paid the last two times!

For a song (UK)

Meaning:

If you buy or sell something for a song, it is very cheap.

Examples of use:

1. I should be able to buy that car **for a song**.

2. That pen is so useless that I wouldn't even buy it **for a song**.

3. I'll give you this watch **for a song** since it's broken.

Forest for the trees

Meaning:

(USA) If someone can't see the **forest for the trees**, they get so caught up in small details that they fail to understand the bigger picture.

Examples of use:

1. Why can't you see the **forest for the trees**? It's a much bigger issue than you think.

2. Some people can't see the **forest for the trees**.

They argue over political parties rather than looking at the potential for war in their respective country.
3. You are never able to see the **forest before the trees**. You worry about minute details rather than looking at the more important points.

From a different angle

Meaning:

If you look at something **from a different angle**, you look at it from a different point of view.

Examples of use:
1. In speech class, you are taught to look at an argument **from a different angle** in order to argue your own point well.
2. Employees that are for a pay rise say that the company's profit is high so we all deserve to benefit. **From a different angle**, the company needs to pay off the loan they got last year.
3. The boy was a bully in school and should be suspended. **From a different angle**, the boy was abused at home and was reaching out to his school.

Full circle

Meaning:

When something has come **full circle**, it has ended

up where it started.

Examples of use:
1. At the very beginning, we picked October 5th as the date for our meeting. After coming up with eight possible dates, we have finally come **full circle** and officially chose the 5th.
2. Jamie dated her first boyfriend for two years. After dating a few other guys over the past six years, Jamie **came full circle** and married her first boyfriend.
3. I originally started my career in engineering. After 10 years in customer service, I've come **full circle** and gone back to engineering.

Gg

Game plan

Meaning:

A **game plan** is a strategy.

Examples of use:
1. Before we have our meeting to persuade our clients to buy our product, we must come up with a **game plan**.
2. In order to teach elementary school students, you must have a **game plan** or else the students will be bored or take advantage of you.
3. The employees wanted more vacation days so before they talked to their boss, they came up with a **game plan** that would convince their boss that they deserved more time off.

Get in on the ground floor

Meaning:

If you **get in on the ground floor**, you enter a project or venture at the start before people know how successful it might be.

Examples of use:
1. People might think you're crazy, but sometimes

it's a good to **get in on the ground floor of a project.**

2. I'm not sure if I'll be making any money from this venture, but I will **get in on the ground floor** and give it a shot.

3. Jack wanted to open a coffee shop. He decided to **get in on the ground floor** and see if it would be profitable or not.

Get off the ground

Meaning:

If a project or plan **gets off the ground**, it starts to be put into operation.

Examples of use:

1. We need to get this project **off the ground** and see where it goes from here.

2. They've been waiting for two months for this property to get sold. If it doesn't **get off the ground soon**, they'll hire another real estate agent.

3. Please **get** your project **off the ground** soon. You've procrastinated long enough.

Get the axe

Meaning:

If you **get the axe**, you lose your job. ('Get the ax' is

the American spelling.)

Examples of use:
1. He **got the axe** after coming late to work seven times last month.
2. If you don't start performing better at work, you'll **get the axe**. This is your first warning.
3. I hate being the boss. I feel bad when my employees **get the axe**. It makes me feel guilty.

Get the ball rolling

Meaning:

If you **get the ball rolling**, you start something so that it can start making progress.

Examples of use:
1. In order to get a driver's license, I better **get the ball rolling** by taking a driver's education course.
2. Lance you've been out of a job for three months. It's time to **get the ball rolling** and apply for some jobs.
3. If we want to do the trade shows in Europe next year, we better **get the ball rolling** and begin planning for the trip.

Get the green light

Meaning:

If you **get the green light** to do something, you are given the necessary permission, authorization.

Examples of use:
1. Beth wanted a new copy machine in the office. Her boss **gave her the green light** to order a new one since the present one was in really bad shape.
2. I just **got the green light** from Harvard University. They accepted me last week!
3. Did you **get the green light** or did Tammy turn down your proposal?

Get the nod

Meaning:

If you **get the nod** to something, you get approval or permission to do it.

Examples of use:
1. The teacher asked the principal if she could buy new curtains for the classroom. The teacher **got the nod** and then bought them the next day.
2. I hope I **get the nod**. I really want that job and I hope that they like me.
3. John asked if he could buy more office supplies for the office if the budget allowed it. He **got the nod** and went to Office Depot the next day.

Get your feet wet

Meaning:

If you **get your feet wet**, you gain your first experience of something.

Examples of use:
1. Some people think that if you want to have a global company, you should **get your feet wet** and start business domestically.
2. Before you start driving, you better **get your feet wet** by having your dad help you practice.
3. I just got this job three days ago, but I'm still **getting my feet wet**. I still have a long way to go before I know all of my duties.

Get your hands dirty

Meaning:

If you **get your hands dirty**, you become involved in something where the realities might compromise your principles. It can also mean that a person is not just stuck in an ivory tower dictating strategy, but is prepared to put in the effort and hard work to make the details actually happen.

Examples of use:

1. Some people think that downloading free music from the internet is **getting their hands dirty**. Although they want to do it, deep down they feel it's wrong.

2. If we want to be successful with this project, we'll just have to **get our hands dirty** and do whatever it takes to get the task finished.

3. If you're afraid to **get your hands dirty**, you'll never succeed. It takes hard work and dedication to get to your goal.

Gift of the gab

Meaning:

If someone has the **gift of the gab**, they speak in a persuasive and interesting way.

Examples of use:

1. Martin has the **gift of the gab**. Just listening to him makes me want to buy his product.

2. I could listen to her all day. She has the **gift of the gab**.

3. She doesn't like boring speakers. She loves people with the **gift of the gab**.

Give someone the runaround

Meaning:

If **someone gives you the runaround**, they make excuses and give you false explanations to avoid doing something.

Examples of use:
1. I'm tired of you **giving me the run around**. Get my car fixed, or else I will take it somewhere else.
2. Matt **gave** Tracy **the run around**. She wanted to find out why he broke up with her but he was too cowardly to be honest about it.
3. Mandy doesn't like to **give** people **the run around**. If she can't get the job done, she will tell the person directly and not make excuses.

Glass ceiling

Meaning:

The **glass ceiling** is the discrimination that prevents women and minorities from getting promoted to the highest levels of companies and organizations.

Examples of use:
1. She wants to be the C.E.O., but she's afraid she can't get past the **glass ceiling**. No woman has been a C.E.O. of that company.
2. I hope this organization doesn't have a **glass ceiling**. I don't want to work five years as a black woman and not get promoted.
3. That company doesn't have a **glass ceiling**.

Anyone with high skills and a good personality has a chance to be successful.

Go against the grain

Meaning:

A person who does things in an unconventional manner, especially if their methods are not generally approved of, is said to **go against the grain**. Such an individual can be called a maverick.

Examples of use:
1. The teacher is very strict and **goes against the grain**. He makes the students do pushups if they disrespect him in class.
2. I may sometimes be too direct to my employees, but if **going against the grain** means a higher working performance, so be it.
3. Having a seminar on the beach definitely **goes against the grain** of a regular traditional seminar.

Go bust

Meaning:

If a company **goes bust**, it goes bankrupt.

Examples of use:
1. The company **went bust** after they were found to

be discriminating against their employees.
2. That bank will **go bust** if they continue to charge so many fees and have continuous poor customer service.
3. Poor sanitation conditions caused that restaurant to **go bust**.

Go for broke

Meaning:

If someone **goes for broke**, they risk everything they have for a potentially greater gain.

Examples of use:
1. Mike really wants that position. He's going to **go for broke** and do whatever it takes to get promoted.
2. I'm **going for broke** and putting all my savings into this business. It's in a great location.
3. Volunteers **go for broke** and work in dangerous countries in order to lead fulfilling lives with joy.

Go south

Meaning:

If things **go south**, they get worse or go wrong.

Examples of use:

1. His health **went south** after working in a polluted environment for so long.
2. Ben hopes his business doesn't **go south** after the economy took a turn for the worse.
3. Their relationship **went south** after she told him she wanted to study abroad.

Go the extra mile

Meaning:

If someone is prepared to **go the extra mile**, they will do everything they can to help or to make something succeed, going beyond their duty what could be expected of them.

Examples of use:
1. Emily **goes the extra mile** at the workplace. She tries to do a good job at work and appreciates her boss a lot.
2. If you want to bring your grade up from a 'C' to a 'B', you need to **go the extra mile** and prove to me that you're serious about studying.
3. The gas station attendant **went the extra mile** by cleaning the driver's windows and giving him a free pack of gum after he filled his gas tank.

Golden handshake

Meaning:

A **golden handshake** is a payment made to someone to get them to leave their job.

Examples of use:
1. The man gave his employee a **golden handshake** by giving him two months salary in order for him to leave the company peacefully.
2. I don't need a **golden handshake**. I can leave without getting a sympathy payment.
3. I heard that Bill's **golden handshake** wasn't that much even after 30 years at the company.

Grab the bull by its horns

Meaning:

If you **grab (take) the bull by its horns**, you deal head-on and directly with a problem.

Examples of use:
1. That team leader has been bullying those workers for the past week. Now is the time to **grab the bull by its horns** so that this problem doesn't get any bigger.
2. The counselor **took the bull by its horns** in order to save the couple's marriage. He got to the bottom of the problem.
3. Instead of just waiting for the problem to get worse, you need to **take the bull by its horns**. Deal

with it and don't be afraid.

Green light

Meaning:

If you are given the **green light**, you are given approval to do something.

Examples of use:
1. I wasn't sure if I could wear shorts on Friday, but my boss gave me the **green light** and said that I could.
2. The manager gave the head of sales the **green light**. If he could prove in the next month that his method was better he could train the others sales teams.
3. Danny wasn't sure if he could invite his friends over to his house for a party while his parents were on vacation. His parents didn't give him the **green light** and he had to wait for them to come back.

Hh

Hard sell

Meaning:

If someone puts a lot of pressure on you to do or buy something, they are **hard selling** it.

Examples of use:
1. Going to a department store can be annoying. The clerks never leave you alone and do a lot of **hard selling**.
2. The car dealer is a **hard seller**. He is very good at convincing people to buy his cars.
3. There's no point in this guy **hard selling** me. I have no interest in that product.

Have the floor

Meaning:

If someone **has the floor**, it is their turn to speak at a meeting.

Examples of use:
1. After Miss Smith speaks, you may then **have the floor**.
2. She finally **had the floor** after listening to her opponent speak for 20 minutes.

3. You now **have the floor** but please keep your speech short.

Have your work cut out

Meaning:

If you **have your work cut out**, you are very busy indeed.

Examples of use:
1. The marketing team **had their work cut out** for them. They had to complete the project in half the normal time.
2. I have three final exams, two presentations, and a paper that are all due in two weeks. I **have my work cut out** for me.
3. Before Jim went on vacation for two weeks, **his work was cut out for him**. He couldn't leave anything unfinished.

Head on the block

Meaning:

If someone's **head is on the block**, they are going to be held responsible and suffer the consequences for something that has gone wrong.

Examples of use:
1. The employee yelled at a customer for not listening to what he was saying. He knew his **head would be on the block** when the manager came back.
2. If you don't get this report done by Friday, your **head will be on the block**.
3. My **head is on the block** because I haven't completed my report.

Hedge your bets

Meaning:

If you **hedge your bets**, you don't risk everything on one opportunity, but try more than one thing.

Examples of use:
1. You should **hedge your bets** instead of focusing on just one job interview. Take as many interviews, so you can and see which one is the best one for you.
2. One way to decide on the perfect marriage partner is to **hedge your bets** and date different people. Dating only one person before you get married may not be the best option.
3. Focusing on one job task at work is not the best way to get a promotion. Why not **hedge your bets** and learn skills in different areas.

Hindsight is twenty-twenty

Meaning:

After something has gone wrong, it is easy to look back and make criticisms.

Examples of use:
1. I shouldn't have broken up with my ex-girlfriend. However, **hindsight is twenty-twenty**.
2. **Hindsight is twenty-twenty**. If I had known then what I know now, I wouldn't have made that big mistake.
3. I really screwed up in the meeting. Since **hindsight is twenty-twenty**, I know exactly what I did wrong now.

Hit and miss

Meaning:

Something that is **hit and miss** is unpredictable and may produce results or may fail.

Examples of use:
1. It's **hit and miss** as to whether Steven will come to the meeting on time. Sometimes he's five minutes early and other times he's 20 minutes late.
2. That restaurant is **hit and miss**. At times we get excellent service, while at other times, you have to chase down the servers.
3. Our sales team is **hit and miss**. We have the best

sales for two quarters and then we have the lowest.

Hit the ground running

Meaning:

If someone **hits the ground running**, they start a new job or position in a very dynamic manner.

Examples of use:
1. Amy **hit the ground running** by bringing in many customers in her first week as the manager of the supermarket. Her changes to the store have really made a difference.
2. Our new nurse has **hit the ground** running in her first day on the job. Many patients have complimented her about how professional she is.
3. I hope the new teacher can **hit the ground running** in his job. I really don't want to babysit him for two months.

Hit the mark

Meaning:

If someone hits the mark, they are right about something.

Examples of use:
1. Sharon really **hit the mark** on that comment. I

totally agree with her.

2. You definitely **hit the mark** with your presentation. There isn't anything I disagreed with and it made complete sense.

3. I didn't think you were right about Martin being a lazy coworker. However, after working with him on a project with him doing very little, you definitely **hit the mark**.

Hold all the aces

Meaning:

If you **hold all the aces**, you have all the advantages and your opponents or rivals are in a weak position.

Examples of use:

1. Our team **holds all the aces**. We have no injuries on our team, while our opponent has two key players that won't be able to play because they're hurt.

2. After coming up with a new innovative invention, the company **holds all the aces** while their rival tries to catch up.

3. Our travel company **holds all the aces**. Our headquarters is located in a prime location with excellent staff, while our opponents just lost their C.E.O. and are restructuring.

Hold water

Meaning:

When you say that something does or does not **'hold water'**, it means that the point of view or argument put forward is or is not sound, strong or logical. For e.g., 'Saying we should increase our interest rates because everyone else is doing so will not hold water'.

Examples of use:
1. Thinking that discipline only happens at home and not at school is an argument that doesn't **hold water**.
2. With more females working as politicians, it's safe to say that any argument that says a woman cannot be a politician doesn't exactly **hold water**.
3. Your proposals definitely **hold water**. You have a lot of evidence and figures to support your claims.

Home stretch

Meaning:

The **home stretch** is the last part of something, like a journey, race or project.

Examples of use:
1. Our project is due in one week. Since we're in the **home stretch**, let's finish strong.
2. I'm in the **home stretch** of my business trip. I can't wait for my flight to touch down in three hours.
3. Dan is in the **home stretch** of his race. He's so

close to victory he can taste it.

Hostile takeover

Meaning:

If a company is bought out when it does not want to be, it is known as a **hostile takeover**.

Examples of use:
1. That restaurant had major health inspection issues, so a **hostile takeover** ensued bringing in a new look with a new owner and new name.
2. In order to kick out that poorly functioning company and for us to move in, we should go for a **hostile takeover**. They're not going to leave willingly.
3. The computer store was a victim of a **hostile takeover**. The city wouldn't allow it to run any more and a new owner was waiting to jump in.

Hot air

Meaning:

Language that is full of words but means little or nothing is hot air.

Examples of use:
1. You're full of **hot air**. I can never believe

anything you say.

2. I hate it when people make promises but never keep them. Their words are nothing but **hot air**.

3. Jackie can't stand her boss. He always tells her she can take a vacation soon, but meetings always come up just before she is able to go. She thinks he's full of **hot air**.

Ii

In the bag

Meaning:

If something is in the bag, it is certain that you will get it or achieve it

Examples of use:
1. The customer signed the contract. Our deal is **in the bag**.
2. Our team is ahead 7-0 in the eighth inning. This game is **in the bag**.
3. This sale is **in the bag**. I'm pretty sure we will hit our target.

In the ballpark

Meaning:

This means that something is close to the adequate or required value.

Examples of use:
1. We offered him a competitive salary. He said we were **in the ballpark**, but is seeking a six-figure deal.
2. Someone called to buy my computer. He offered me $200 for it. Although he's **in the ballpark**, I

would really like him to give me $300.

3. I want to buy that house. I offered the real estate agent $250,000 for the house. Since I'm **in the ballpark**, she said she would talk to the owner and find out if that offer will be sufficient.

In the black

Meaning:

If your bank account is in credit, it is **in the black**.

Examples of use:

1. It's so nice not to be in debt, but to be **in the black**.

2. I'm tired of our company losing money. Let's get **in the black** by restructuring everything including the staff, spending plan, and objectives.

3. Good news! Even after paying a lot of taxes, your business is still **in the black** and continuing to make a profit.

In the hole

Meaning:

If someone is in the hole, they have a lot of problems, especially financial ones.

Examples of use:
1. If we don't get **out of this hole** soon, we'll have to declare bankruptcy.
2. John and Katie are **in the hole** after spending $50,000 on their credit cards but not being able to pay it off.
3. If you want to succeed in business, you need to get **out of the hole that you're in**. You won't be able to survive with so much debt.

In the know

Meaning:

If you are **in the know**, you have access to all the information about something, which other people don't have.

Examples of use:
1. The vice president is **in the know** of what the C.E.O. does. He knows all the plans the C.E.O. has because of his trust in him.
2. I want to be the person **in the know** and have others depend on me to find out what's going on in the company.
3. Why is she always **in the know** at the company? I don't know how she always finds out what's happening in our office.

In the loop

Meaning:

If you're **in the loop**, you are fully informed about what is happening in a certain area or activity.

Examples of use:
1. Please keep me **in the loop**. I don't want to be the last one to know what's happening.
2. Kelly is always **in the loop** at work. She communicates with her boss well and knows what is expected of her every day.
3. Since I live so far away from my family, I'm never **in the loop** with what's going on with my brothers and sisters.

In the making

Meaning:

When something is **in the making**, it means it is in the process of being made.

Examples of use:
1. This movie is **in the making**. By this time next year, it will be finished.
2. I hope those cookies are **in the making**. We have our big Thanksgiving meal tomorrow and we need those cookies for the dessert.
3. The deal is **in the making**. We should have an agreement by next week.

In the pipeline

Meaning:

If something's **in the pipeline**, it hasn't arrived yet but its arrival is expected.

Examples of use:
1. We have our new teacher **in the pipeline**. He should be able to start next week.
2. My paperwork is **in the pipeline**. The government just sent my criminal background check information two days ago.
3. I wired the invoice payment to your account two hours ago. It's **in the pipeline** and should be in your account by tomorrow morning.

In the red

Meaning:

If your bank account is overdrawn, it is in the red.

Examples of use:
1. If I don't get a job, my bank account will soon be **in the red**.
2. After the economic slowdown, our company's bank account went **into the red** because of slow sales.
3. We need to get **out of the red**. Start pushing the

sales team or we will be in trouble.

Jj

Jockey for position

Meaning:

If a number of people want the same opportunity and are struggling to emerge as the most likely candidate, they are **jockeying for position**.

Examples of use:
1. So many highly qualified accountants are **jockeying for position**, but we can only hire one since we don't have a big enough budget for more.
2. Four engineers are **jockeying for position** to work at the most prestigious I.T. Company.
3. All of the flight attendants know how to handle passengers and seem very professional. After all of them have been **jockeying for the senior position**, it's hard to choose.

Just for the record

Meaning:

If something is said to be **just for the record**, the person is saying it so that people know but does not necessarily agree with or support it.

Examples of use:
1. My opponent said that he doesn't support term

limits. **Just for the record**, I don't agree with that.
2. The city council said that we need to hire more police officers. **Just for the record**, I'm not sure if I support it since we don't have the budget for more law enforcement.
3. He said that she was a terrible chef. **Just for the record**, I think she makes excellent food and I would love for her to work in my restaurant.

Kk

Keep your ear to the ground

Meaning:

If you **keep your ear to the ground**, you try to keep informed about something, especially if there are rumors or uncertainties.

Examples of use:
1. The boss has been very secretive. I need to **keep my ear to the ground** to make sure I know what's going on in the office.
2. There were rumors that are company was going to be sold to another owner. Let's **keep our ear to the ground**, so that we're prepared to leave if we have to.
3. When that department talk in the cafeteria, we should **keep our ears to the ground** in order to find out what they are planning.

Keep your head above water

Meaning:

If you are just managing to survive financially, you are **keeping your head above water**.

Examples of use:
1. After having three kids and getting a cut in pay,

I'm just **keeping my head above water**. I might need to get a part time job too.

2. Some people wonder why teachers only just **keep their heads above water**, while baseball players are wealthy.

3. Since the family business went bankrupt, John and his wife Cindy are having a hard time **keeping their heads above water**.

Keep your options open

Meaning:

If someone's **keeping their options open**, they aren't going to restrict themselves or rule out any possible course of action.

Examples of use:

1. Because Jackie isn't sure if she wants a long term relationship with me yet, I'm **keeping my options open** and going to keep dating other women.

2. You could transfer our company to Los Angeles or San Diego. Just **keep your options open** and see which one will be a better choice down the line.

3. Now that we have some extra cash from investors, we can **keep our options open** on which equipment to purchase.

Kill the goose that lays the golden egg

Meaning:

If you **kill the goose that lays the golden egg**, you ruin something that is very profitable.

Examples of use:
1. Why did we change this product? Now that we did, we **killed the goose that laid the golden egg**. No one wants to buy it any more.
2. One way to **kill the goose that lays the golden egg** is to try to cut corners by trying to save money.
3. Coca Cola almost **killed the goose that laid the golden egg**. Fortunately, they went back to the original formula and got their customers back.

Knee-jerk reaction

Meaning:

A **knee-jerk reaction** is an instant, instinctive response to a situation.

Examples of use:
1. **Knee-jerk reactions** can be dangerous because you do something without thinking.
2. My sister is investing in a risky new stock. My **knee-jerk reaction** is to tell her to rethink her strategy but it's her money.
3. If a competitor comes out with a new product, a **knee-jerk reaction** would be to make an

advertisement and criticize it. A wiser move would be to work on a better product.

Know the ropes

Meaning:

Someone who is experienced and knows how the system works **know the ropes**.

Examples of use:
1. After working in the office for six months, Marcy now **knows the ropes** and can teach new employees how to work there.
2. If you have any questions, ask Steve. He's been in the company for 20 years and **knows the ropes** really well.
3. I hope she **knows the ropes**. I don't want to have to train another rookie again.

Ll

Let's call it a day

Meaning:

This is used as a way of suggesting that it is time to stop working on something.

Examples of use:
1. After working 12 hours, it's time to **call it a day**. I need to go home and rest.
2. **Let's call it a day**. We worked enough today and I'm hungry!
3. Thanks for all your help with the meeting and all your hard work today. **Let's call it a day** and I'll see you tomorrow!

Level playing field

Meaning:

If there's a **level playing field** everybody is treated equally.

Examples of use:
1. Amy is a great C.E.O. She works with a **level playing field** in her company. Everyone is treated with equal respect.
2. In some companies women feel like they're not on

a **level playing field** and have to prove themselves a lot more than men.

3. If a boss doesn't have a **level playing field** in the office, no one will respect each other.

Light at the end of the tunnel

Meaning:

If you can see **light at the end of the tunnel**, then you can see some signs of hope in the future, though things are difficult at the moment.

Examples of use:
1. After struggling at the beginning of the semester, I see **light at the end of the tunnel** after getting an 'A' on the midterm exam.
2. Nancy can see **light at the end of the tunnel**. After years of drinking, her husband hasn't had a drink in over two weeks.
3. I just got a major raise at work. I had been worried about being able to afford a home, but now I see **light at the end of the tunnel**.

Light bulb moment

Meaning:

A **light bulb moment** is when you have a sudden realization about something, like the light bulbs that used to indicate an idea in cartoons.

Examples of use:
1. Carson experienced a **light bulb moment** and knows what he should do to keep his employees motivated.
2. It's always great to get a **light bulb moment** during a negotiation. Just when you think you the deal is almost lost, you turn it around.
3. He wasn't sure how to do the quotation. However, he had a **light bulb moment** and was able to complete it.

Loan shark

Meaning:

A **loan shark** lends money at very high rates of interest.

Examples of use:
1. Never borrow money from a **loan shark**. You probably won't be able to repay the debt.
2. I know the company is desperate for money, but I can't believe you suggested going to a **loan shark**.
3. As a **loan shark** you can make a lot of money, but people will hate you.

Long shot

Meaning:

If something is a **long shot**, there is only a very small chance of success.

Examples of use:
1. It's a real **long shot**, but we need to try or we'll be bankrupt.
2. I know it's a **long shot**, but it's worth the risk to get the deal.
3. This is too much of a **long shot**, we should stop now before we regret it.

Loose cannon

Meaning:

A person who is very difficult to control and unpredictable is a **loose cannon**.

Examples of use:
1. She is very careful not to spend too much time with him at the office. He's a **loose cannon** and loses his temper very easily.
2. The sales manager didn't want to have a **loose cannon** in his department. He needed someone that was calm temper and would listen to the customers.
3. I wouldn't want to have a boss that was a **loose cannon**. I would be scared to go to work.

Lower the bar

Meaning:

If people change the standards required to make things easier, they **lower the bar**.

Examples of use:
1. Some states have **lowered the bar** on education, so that many people will pass the test but with a lot fewer expectations.
2. We've **lowered the bar** on this one too much. We won't make any profit.
3. Perfection is good, but hard to achieve. We need to **lower the bar** otherwise we will never start production.

Lower your sights

Meaning:

If you **lower your sights**, you accept something that is less than you were hoping for.

Examples of use:
1. Don't be so picky. **Lower your sights** and enjoy the food!
2. We shouldn't **lower our sights** in order get production finished. Quality is a must for this design.
3. I have to **lower my sights** if I want to get hired quickly.

Mm

Make a killing

Meaning:

If you **make a killing**, you do something that makes you a lot of money.

Examples of use:
1. These cookies taste great. Sell them so you can **make a killing**!
2. Good technological companies' **make a killing** by coming out with new phones all the time.
3. Cosmetics companies **make a killing** off of young women in their 20s.

Make a pitch

Meaning:

If you **make a pitch** for something, you make a bid, offer or other attempt to get it.

Examples of use:
1. If you want to buy that company, you need to **make a pitch** and be aggressive.
2. If you **make a pitch** like that on your business trips, we won't get any deals.
3. Have you **made a pitch** to them yet? You know

we're depending on this deal don't you?

Make ends meet

Meaning:

If somebody finds it hard to **make ends meet**, they have problems living on the money they earn.

Examples of use:
1. We need to stop spending on things we don't need, so that we can **make ends meet**.
2. We can purchase from them at a low price, because they are having difficulty **making ends meet**. They need our money.
3. In order to **make ends meet**, the company started to sell off their assets.

Make headway

Meaning:

If you **make headway**, you make progress.

Examples of use:
1. She **made headway** on her report. She predicts she'll be done in a couple of hours.
2. Brandon wants to **make headway** on his sales target. He'll be overtime from tomorrow.
3. Patricia has so much paperwork waiting on her

desk. She's not **making any headway** on it.

Make money hand over fist

Meaning:

If you **make money hand over fist**, you make a lot of money without any difficulty.

Examples of use:
1. He's such a great telemarketer, that he **makes money hand over fist**. He's on his way to being wealthy in a very short amount of time.
2. Most people would love to just work at home and **make money hand over fist**. Unless they have a special talent, that's almost impossible to do.
3. Sales people **make money hand over fist** in this company. That's why they never leave.

Meet someone halfway

Meaning:

If you **meet someone halfway,** you accept some of their ideas and make concessions.

Examples of use:
1. Don't be so stubborn. **Meet me halfway** and compromise with me.

2. If you don't **meet me halfway**, negotiations will be off the table. I can't stand someone that is selfish and only thinks about himself.

3. I offered $50 to buy that jacket. The clerk said to pay him $60. We both **met each other halfway** and I paid him $55.

Money talks

Meaning:

Money talks means that people can convey many messages with money, and many things can be discovered about people by observing the way they use their money.

Examples of use:

1. He really liked this company but **money talks**. He started working in a new organization last week.

2. Yes, **money does talk**. Corruption in business is common here.

3. If you want me to help you edit your book, I can do that. However, **money talks** and I need some kind of compensation for doing that much work.

Nn

Need no introduction

Meaning:
Someone who is very famous and known to everyone **needs no introduction**.

Examples of use:
1. This man **needs no introduction**. He invented the most innovative smart phone in history.
2. Ladies and gentleman, a man that **needs no introduction**: John McLeod!
3. I would like to introduce my next guest but she really **needs no introduction** due to her amazing career.

Nine-to-five

Meaning:
Nine-to-five is a job during normal working hours. The term came into existence because many work days start at 9 AM and end at 5 PM.

Examples of use:

1. She was tired of working a **nine-to-five** job, so she got a job at a restaurant.
2. I just want a regular **nine-to-five** job. I'm tired of working the graveyard shift.

3. John wanted an exciting job. He didn't want a **nine-to-five** job where he sits at the computer all day and answers phones.

No brainer

Meaning:
If a decision is really obvious or really easy to make, the decision is a **no brainer**.

Examples of use:
1. Taking the job was a **no brainer**. The salary was higher, more vacation days were offered, and I got an expense account.
2. Tammy's decision to leave her boyfriend was a **no brainer**. He never treated her right and didn't seem to love her.
3. Changing careers was a **no brainer**. Although changing my job was hard I hated the direction was going in.

Nothing ventured, nothing gained

Meaning:
Nothing ventured, nothing gained means if you don't try to do something, you'll never succeed

Examples of use:

1. It's risky to spend so much time developing a new brand, but **nothing ventured, nothing gained**.
2. Chris said he's not sure how much our boss will like our new product ideas, but **nothing ventured, nothing gained**.
3. We're not sure if expanding our business abroad will help us succeed or not, but **nothing ventured, nothing gained**.

No strings attached

Meaning:
If something is given without expecting anything in return, it is given with **no strings attached**.

Examples of use:
1. They will let you test drive the car for free. There are **no strings attached**. They won't try to persuade you to buy it.
2. Mike didn't want to have a serious relationship with Dana. He just wanted **no strings attached**.
3. You can have that day off. There are **no strings attached**. I just want to give you time with your family.

No time to lose

Meaning:
If there is **no time to lose**, it means that there is a lot of pressure to complete something quickly.

Examples of use:
1. I asked them to send the email by the end of the day. It's already 4:45pm and I need to get home. There's **no time to lose**.
2. There's **no time to lose**. We have to start winning contracts. There are only two weeks left in the sales quarter.
3. Two other companies are looking for employees. There's **no time to lose**. Employ him now!

Not going to fly

Meaning:
If a solution isn't effective, people say that it **isn't going to fly**.

Examples of use:
1. I don't think his idea is **going to fly**. Let's keep generating more possibilities.
2. That's **not going to fly** with me. You can't take my client out for dinner alone.
3. Chris wanted to ask his boss for a day off. But he had just been on holiday for two weeks, so it probably wasn't **going to fly**.

Null and void

Meaning:

If something's **null and void**, it is invalid or is no longer applicable

Examples of use:
1. This coupon expired last month. It's now **null and void**.
2. Your third car accident in three months has caused your insurance policy to be **null and void**.
3. Clause 3.1 in your contract makes that **null and void**.

Number cruncher

Meaning:
A **number cruncher** is an accountant or someone who is very good at dealing with numbers and calculations

Examples of use:
1. I'm really bad at math. I'll leave it to the **number cruncher** to help me with the budget.
2. She can calculate my taxes really quickly. She's a real **number cruncher**.
3. We should ask the **number cruncher** to figure out our profits and expenditures. I don't want to spend all day doing it.

Nuts and bolts

Meaning:
The **nuts and bolts** are the most essential components of something

Examples of use:
1. There is a meeting on Saturday but I need to know the **nuts and bolts** of the proposal, so I can be prepared for it.
2. If you want to succeed in your future goals, you need to figure out the **nuts and bolts** first, so you can meet it realistically.
3. Writing a report is difficult, but if I know the **nuts and bolts** about the subject it's no problem.

Oo

Off the chart

Meaning:
If something goes **off the chart**, it far exceeds the normal standards, good or bad, for something

Examples of use:
1. That speech was **off the chart**. I can't believe how well that guy presented his argument.
2. "Speed 2" was so bad, it went **off the chart** and didn't even make the list of bad movies.
3. Edward's performance is **off the chart**. He goes above and beyond by doing more than what is expected of him.

Off the mark

Meaning:
If something is **off the mark**, it is inaccurate or incorrect

Examples of use:
1. His assessment of our rivals' ability was completely **off the mark**.
2. Your projected sales figures were way **off the mark**. I doubt you'll get a bonus this year.
3. His argument was **off the mark**. The audience booed for 10 minutes after his controversial remarks.

Off the record

Meaning:
Something **off the record** is said in confidence because the speaker doesn't want it attributed to them, especially when talking to the media.

Examples of use:
1. Please keep this **off the record**. I wouldn't want CNN to find out how I really feel about our rival company.
2. Since we are in a city that heavily favors Democratic candidates, let's keep it **off the record** that I support the Republican senator's re-election bid.
3. I know you have a good relationship with the boss, but **off the record** I want to say how incapable he is.

Off the shelf

Meaning:
If a product is **off the shelf**, it can be used straightaway without any setting-up

Examples of use:
1. You can buy this lamp **off the shelf**. You don't have to assemble it.
2. An iMac is a great **off the shelf** product. All you have to do is plug it in.

3. I can sell this cell phone **off the shelf**. The power is on and ready to use.

Off the top of one's head

Meaning:
If someone says something **off the top of his or her head**, it means that he or she gives a response without thinking about it for a long time or doing any research on the subject.

Examples of use:
1. **Off the top of my head**, I believe there's a good Italian restaurant on Main Street.
2. With regards to the percentage of returns, I would say **off the top of my head** that we need to watch production.
3. **Off the top of my head**, I heard that the company was interested in investing in our product.

On a roll

Meaning:
If you're **on a roll**, you're moving from success to success

Examples of use:
1. Jenny got job offers from three companies. She's **on a roll**.

2. The Red Sox are **on a roll**. They've won eight games in a row.
3. He's been promoted three times in the past year. He's **on a** serious **roll**.

On good terms

Meaning:
If people are **on good terms**, they have a good relationship

Examples of use:
1. Despite Steve Jobs and Bill Gates being rivals in the past, they tried to stay **on good terms** with each other to avoid conflict.
2. Mike's boss knows that he does a good job at work. Because of that they're both **on good terms** with each other.
3. Different sales teams aren't usually **on good terms** because of their rivalry.

On hold

Meaning:
If something is **on hold**, no action is being taken

Examples of use:
1. While on the phone, the operator put Jim **on hold** and made him wait 30 minutes to talk to someone.

2. The business trip is put **on hold** until after our boss recovers from his surgery this week.

3. The deal was put **on hold** because they need more funding.

On ice

Meaning:
If plans are put **on ice**, they are delayed and no action will be taken for the foreseeable future

Examples of use:
1. The deal between the owner and players was put **on ice** due to a salary disagreement. The strike continued.

2. We'll have to put our travel plans **on ice** until my job gives me a raise. We just don't have enough money at the moment.

3. We need to put this project **on ice** until we are sure that we have the finances.

On the level

Meaning:
If someone is honest and trustworthy, they are **on the level**

Examples of use:

1. John is **on the level**. As a mechanic, he never overcharges his customers and never recommends repairs that the customers don't need.
2. I appreciate my lawyer for being **on the level**. Despite my court case being delayed three times, he rarely charged me for extra attorney's fees.
3. I'm **on the level** with my staff. That way they always work hard for me.

On the line

Meaning:
If somebody's job is **on the line**, they stand a very good chance of losing it

Example of use:
1. After coming to work drunk for the last two days, Marge found her job **on the line**.
2. If you arrive late again, your job will be **on the line** and you'll be given a written warning.
3. Chris's job was **on the line** after he yelled at the boss over a really small matter.

On the same wavelength

Meaning:
If people are **on the same wavelength**, they have the same ideas and opinions about something

Examples of use:

1. Thank goodness my coworker and I are **on the same wavelength** about sharing the office duties, or we would argue all the time.
2. When it comes to cleaning the house, my wife and I are always **on the same wavelength**. We always agree every time.
3. James is always **on the same wavelength** as his boss. They communicate well together.

On the shelf

Meaning:
If something like a project is **on the shelf**, nothing is being done about it at the moment

Examples of use:
1. My internship has been put **on the shelf** because I have to take care of my mother, who broke her leg after skiing.
2. The architects put their building project **on the shelf** until the city passed a law asking for the taxpayers to fund it.
3. His plans to write the company manual are **on the shelf** until he can find the time.

On the take

Meaning (UK):
Someone who is stealing from work is **on the take**

Examples of use:
1. He's been **on the take** for years. He takes office supplies from work and sells them.
2. Kelly is **on the take**. She thinks nobody has noticed, but it's just a matter of time before the boss knows.
3. I was **on the take** at work for ages. I'm surprised nobody noticed.

One-man band (or one-man show)

Meaning:
If one person does all the work or has all the responsibility somewhere, then they are a **one-man band**

Examples of use:
1. Our teacher asked the three of us to do a group presentation but because no one else was helping me, I felt like a **one-man band**.
2. She does all the work in the office while everyone else is lazy. She's a **one-man band**.
3. He's a **one-man band**. No-one else can reach his sales figures.

Out of pocket

Meaning:

If you are **out of pocket** on a deal, you have lost money

Examples of use:
1. She thought buying her house would be a good investment. However, she was **out of pocket** on the deal a year later.
2. Don't buy that company. You might be **out of pocket** before you know it.
3. Our company invested a lot of money in that project. When the city changed their mind we were **out of pocket** by thousands of dollars.

Out of the box

Meaning:
Thinking **out of the box** is thinking in a creative way. However, it can also be used for a ready-made product that requires no specialist knowledge to set it up

Examples of use:
1. This is an **out of the box** product. No assembly is required. All you have to do is plug it in.
2. We must think **outside the box** and not just have the same ideas as everyone else if we want this product to sell.
3. I don't want my presentation to be boring. I better think **outside the box**.

Over the counter

Meaning:

Medicines and drugs that can be sold without a doctor's prescription are sold **over the counter**

Examples of use:
1. You don't need a prescription for Tylenol. You can get it **over the counter**.
2. Prozac is not **over the counter**. You need to talk to a psychiatrist and ask if they think it would be beneficial to you.
3. The pharmacy makes most of its profit from **over the counter** medicine.

Pp

Pass the buck

Meaning:
If you **pass the buck**, you avoid taking responsibility by saying that someone else is responsible

Examples of use:
1. The journalist made a mistake and put the wrong name into the news article making the boss very angry. The journalist then **passed the buck** and said that he was given the wrong information.
2. The sales team underachieved during the second quarter. They **passed the buck** and said that the product was the problem, not them.
3. Employees should never **pass the buck** onto their coworkers when they themselves make mistakes. They will lose integrity that way.

Pay off a loan

Meaning:

To **pay off a loan** is to finish paying off money borrowed from a bank, business, or person

Examples of use:

1. I have $20,000 left from my university loans. I hope I can **pay** it **off** within the next five years.
2. Sir, you need to **pay off the loan** on your car or else your interest will jump 5%.
3. We have finished **paying off our loan** now our accounts are in the black.

Pay through the nose

Meaning:
If you **pay through the nose** for something, you pay a very high price for it

Examples of use:
1. Don't **pay through the nose** for auto insurance. There are cheaper options everywhere.
2. Our accountants are useless. We always **pay through the nose** on our taxes.
3. Many people are willing to **pay through the nose** for new gadgets, but not willing to donate a penny to charity.

Pecking order

Meaning:
The **pecking order** is the order of importance or rank

Examples of use:

1. The C.E.O., president, vice president, and employees make up the **pecking order**.
2. Tim wants to move up the **pecking order** at work, so he can get more respect and money.
3. Before you yell at me, remember the **pecking order**. I'm above you so you have to listen to me.

Pencil somebody or something in

Meaning:

When you **pencil somebody in** you write in something with a pencil (implies that the writing is not final)

Examples of use:
1. We **penciled** you **in** for Monday the 22nd for your doctor's appointment.
2. A date has already been **penciled in**, but we can change it easily.
3. She was **penciled in** to give a presentation, but she had to cancel.

Phase something out

Meaning:

If we **phase something out** we gradually stop providing or using something

Examples of use:
1. Several manufacturers are **phasing out** dangerous working conditions.
2. The company plans to **phase** the system **out** within the next three years.
3. That glue is really messy. Let's **phase** this one **out** and make a better one.

Piece of the action

Meaning:
A **piece of the action** is a share in the activity or profits of something

Examples of use:
1. What is everyone talking about? I don't want to be left out. Give me a **piece of the action** too.
2. That company's stocks have gone up in the last six months. Let's get a **piece of the action** before the stocks drop.
3. Rick, we're going to a baseball game on Friday. Do you want a **piece of the action** too?

Play catch up

Meaning:
Play catch up is when you make a big effort to overcome a late start; when you are behind and have

to take actions to get to the level of your competition.

Examples of Use:
1. Manchester United had to **play catch up** after being down two goals within the first five minutes.
2. Microsoft had to **play catch up** in the music industry of technology when Apple came out with iPods.
3. Amy sold 45 more computers than John last month. John is **playing catch up** this month to try and attempt to level the competition.

Play hardball

Meaning:
To **play hardball** means to be competitive in a cruel way and without showing mercy. **Playing hardball** means doing anything possible to win.

Examples of use:
1. Steve is a great guy, but I'm going to get more clients than him. All I have to do is **play** some **hardball**.
2. If you want to defeat that team, you need to aim for the quarterback. We need to **play hardball** to have a chance to win.
3. Amy is interested in that promotion, but so am I. I'm going to **play hardball**, so she doesn't get it.

Play second fiddle

Meaning:

If you **play second fiddle**, you take a subordinate role behind someone more important

Examples of use:
1. Tracy is tired of **playing second fiddle**. Her boss likes her coworker while Tracy gets most of the work.
2. The sales division will always **play second fiddle** to the marketing department when it comes to budget allowance.
3. She doesn't mind **playing second fiddle** in the company if that means that her coworker brings in more sales

Plug a product

Meaning:

When we **plug a product** we promote a product; we talk positively about it

Examples of use:
1. American Express use famous people to **plug** their credit cards. No wonder people pay attention to their ads.

2. While having an interview with the late night talk show host, the author **plugged** his book so people would go out and buy it.

3. When Jim came over for dinner, we found out that he was a kitchen knife salesman. He wouldn't stop **plugging** them to us.

Pressed for time

Meaning:
If you are **pressed for time**, you are in a hurry or working against a very tight schedule

Examples of use:
1. Sorry gentlemen. I'm a bit **pressed for time**. I need to leave now if I want to make it to my next meeting without being late.

2. The woman was **pressed for time** when she was on her way to work. She ran to catch the subway.

3. Jonathan hates being **pressed for time**. He always arrives 30 minutes early for meetings.

Pros and cons

Meaning:
Pros and cons are arguments for or against a particular issue. Pros are arguments which aim to promote the issue, while cons suggest points against it. The term has been in use since the 16th century

and is a shortening of a Latin phrase, pro et contra, which means "for and against." Considering the **pros and cons** of an issue is a very useful way to weigh the issue thoughtfully and reach an informed decision.

Examples of use:
1. Before deciding on constructing a building in downtown, we need to look at the **pros and cons**.
2. A healthy debate looks at both sides of the issues, the **pros and the cons**.
3. What are the **pros and cons** of going into business with family?

Pull out all the stops

Meaning:
If you **pull out all the stops**, you do everything you possibly can to achieve the result you want

Examples of use:
1. Chris was very persistent and **pulled out all the stops** in order to get the job that he wanted.
2. We need to match our sales quota by tomorrow. Go out there, **pull out all the stops**, and sell as many products as you can.
3. Jason **pulled out the stops** to get the job of his dreams.

Pull the plug

Meaning:

If you **pull the plug** you put a stop to a project or initiative, usually because it's not going well; to stop something from moving forward; to discontinue

Examples of use:
1. After losing millions of dollars when drilling oil in Oklahoma, the oil company finally **pulled the plug** on the project.
2. Due to so many hurricanes happening along the East Coast, the hotel chain decided to **pull the plug** on building on the coastline.
3. The basketball player failed his physical exam. Therefore the team that was interested in him **pulled the plug** on the deal.

Pull the trigger

Meaning:
The person who **pulls the trigger** is the one who does the action that closes or finishes something

Examples of use:
1. If you want to close that deal, you better **pull the trigger** before you lose that client to someone else.
2. Daniel almost hesitated and didn't **pull the trigger** on signing the contract.
3. Michael Jordan was good at **pulling the trigger**. He always finished his goals.

Pull your weight

Meaning:

If someone is not **pulling their weight**, they aren't making enough effort, especially in group work.

Examples of use:
1. Brad was so angry because he did most of the work while his coworkers just sat around and surfed the internet. His coworkers weren't **pulling their weight**.
2. We need you to **pull your weight** at the office or else we will find someone to replace you.
3. Some students don't enjoy doing a group presentation because one or two of the students might be doing most of the work, while the others don't **pull their weight** and take credit for it.

Push a product

Meaning:

To promote a product

Examples of use:
1. Proctor and Gamble **push** a lot of their detergent products such as 'Tide' on TV to get more customers.

2. Some people hate it when toy companies **push their products** in commercials when kids are watching cartoons.

3. If we want to sell more electronics, we should **push our product** in men's magazines and sports sections of newspapers.

Put all your eggs in one basket

Meaning:

If you **put all your eggs in one basket**, you risk everything on a single opportunity which, like eggs breaking, could go wrong.

Examples of use:

1. **Putting all your eggs into one basket** is dangerous when investing. You might lose it all if you invest all your money into one company.

2. If you save up all of your money to open a coffee shop, don't **put all of your eggs in that basket**. Save some of your money in case the business fails.

3. I have three job options. I really like one position. But I'm afraid if I **put all of my eggs in one basket**, I could lose the other two opportunities.

Put a stake in the ground

Meaning:

If you **put a stake in the ground** you take the first step; to make a move to get something started; to make commitment

Examples of use:
1. Our business in this county has grown steadily over the last two years. Now it's time to **put a stake in the ground** and put our headquarters here.
2. Let's **put a stake in the ground** and start our long term business together.
3. If we want to be serious about marriage, we should **put a stake in the ground** and get engaged.

Put you in the picture

Meaning:

If you **put someone in the picture**, you tell them the information they need to know about something.

Examples of use:
1. Let me **put you in the picture**. If John doesn't work harder, he'll be fired.
2. I need to **put** the boss **in the picture** and report the accident that happened in the factory to him.
3. Kevin's grades have been slipping. The teacher will have to **put** the parents **in the picture**.

Put your heads together

Meaning:

If people **put their heads together**, they exchange ideas about something.

Examples of use:
1. Our trip to Australia is next month. Let's **put our heads together** and come up with an itinerary.
2. Our rivals are stealing our customers. We need to **put our heads together** and come up with a plan to change that.
3. Donna regularly loses contracts. We need to **put our heads together** and find out why.

Put someone on hold

Meaning:

When you **put someone on hold** you disconnect them temporarily while you do something else

Examples of use:
1. Please don't **put me on hold**. I've already been waiting 30 minutes to get someone to help me solve my problem.
2. The lines were all busy. Jennifer was **put on hold** by the operator for 15 minutes.
3. Sir, let me **put you on hold** for a second while I check to see if your wife is in the office.

Put the cart before the horse

Meaning:
To **put the cart before the horse** means to do or think about things in the wrong way.

Examples of use:
1. They were trying to find investors without having a business plan. They were **putting the cart before the horse**.
2. Mark bought an engagement ring for a girl he just met. He **put the cart before the horse**.
3. Don't **put the cart before the horse**. Get your degree first and then look for a job.

Put your money where your mouth is

Meaning:

If someone **puts their money where their mouth is**, they back up their words with action.

Examples of use:
1. **Put your money where your mouth is** and come to my wedding.
2. You say you want to sign this contract. If that's the case, then **put your money where your mouth is**.

3. Don't just tell me that you're going to sell $1000 worth of products today. **Put your money where your mouth is** and show me.

Qq

Quick buck

Meaning:

If you make some money easily, you make a **quick buck**.

Examples of use:
1. Our company needs to make a **quick buck** to pay off these bills.
2. In order to make a **quick buck**, you should target customers that are most interested in this product.
3. What's the best way for me to make a **quick buck**? I want to buy a new car.

Quick off the mark

Meaning:

If someone is **quick off the mark**, they are very quick to use, start or do something new.

Examples of use:
1. Edward is **quick off the mark**. Despite today being his first day at work, he's adjusted quickly.
2. My sister is **quick off the mark** in marathons. She is always ahead of her competitors at the beginning of the race.

3. Jim's boss wants his employees to be **quick off the mark**. As soon as they arrive at the office, he wants them to start working on their projects so that they can go home on time.

Rr

Raw deal

Meaning:

If you get a **raw deal**, you are treated unfairly.

Examples of use:
1. You want me to pay $5000 for this 10-year old jalopy? That's a **raw deal**.
2. My boss is giving me a **raw deal**. He wants me to go on a business trip and give a presentation, while my coworker stays in the office and does paperwork.
3. Dad, why does Bobby get to have his own room, while I have to share a bedroom with Amy? I think that's a **raw deal**.

Read between the lines

Meaning:
To **read between the lines** means to understand something that wasn't communicated directly.
Reading between the lines involves understanding what someone is implying or suggesting but not saying directly.

Examples of use:

1. He didn't say that he wanted to leave the company. However after **reading between the lines**, I could tell that he wanted to quit.
2. The woman isn't answering your text messages. **Read between the lines**. She isn't interested in you.
3. You should **read between the lines**. Even though the boss didn't tell you he was upset that you were late, he hasn't talked to you all day.

Red tape

Meaning:

Red tape is a negative term for the official paperwork and bureaucracy that we have to deal with.

Examples of use:
1. For some countries' citizens, they have to go through a lot of **red tape** to become a U.S. citizen.
2. It's getting easier to get a driver's license. There is less **red tape** to get through. I just have to fill out one form now.
3. In order to become a politician, you may have to get through a lot of **red tape** before you finally achieve your goal.

Reinvent the wheel

Meaning:

If someone **reinvents the wheel**, they waste their time doing something that has already been done by other people, when they could be doing something more worthwhile.

Examples of Use:
1. We don't need to **reinvent the wheel**. There are already MP3 players on the market. We don't need to come up with another version.
2. There's no sense in coming up with a smart phone with a small screen. That's like **reinventing the wheel** since it's already been done before.
3. Writing a book about relationships between men and women has been done too many times. There's no reason to **reinvent the wheel**.

Rip someone off

Meaning:

To **rip someone off** is to deprive somebody by deceit

Examples of use:
1. The clerk charged me $150 for my winter coat. When I walked down the street, I found the same coat for $90. He totally **ripped me off**.
2. Kelly feels like she's been **ripped off** when she pays a lot of money for food.

3. I don't want to go to the concert. If I have to pay a lot of money for a bad seat, I'll feel like I've been **ripped off**.

Roll something out

Meaning:

If you **roll something out** you officially launch a new product or service

Examples of use:
1. The car manufacturer will **roll out** its new model next year.
2. They are able to **roll** new products **out** every six months.
3. The coffee will be tested in Asia and it will be **rolled out** in the U.S. soon thereafter.

Round something up (to something)

Meaning:

When we **round something up** we increase an amount to the next higher whole number

Examples of use:
1. John and Mike **rounded up** the price to $860.

2. It's easier to **round** these figures **up** in fives or tens.
3. The total came out to $397.87 but I will just **round** it **up** to $400.

Round-the-clock

Meaning:
If a company has **round-the-clock** service, it means they are open 24 hours a day.

Examples of use:
1. It's 1am and I'm hungry. I'm sure there's a fast food restaurant that's open **round-the-clock**.
2. Doctors have to work **round-the-clock** during emergency situations.
3. If you want to be a truck driver, get ready to drive **round-the-clock** to deliver heavy loads of freight.

Rule of thumb

Meaning:

Rule of thumb means an estimation made according to a rough and ready practical rule, not based on science or exact measurement.

Examples of use:

1. It's my **rule of thumb** to never work with family. It's just not a wise thing to do.
2. Selling reliable products at a low price should be every company's **rule of thumb**.
3. An important **rule of thumb** is to treat your business clients well. Then you'll have a solid long-term relationship.

Run it past someone

Meaning:

To ask someone his/her opinion about something and find out what the person says about it is to **run it past someone**.

Examples of use:
1. I think we should hire two more cashiers at the store, but I'll **run it past** the manager and see what he thinks.
2. Before you make your vacation plans, **run it past** the boss to get his approval first.
3. Did you **run** the idea **past** the department head before you put it into action?

Run something into the ground

Meaning:

If people **run something into the ground**, they treat or manage it so badly that they ruin it.

Examples of use:
1. The owner of the restaurant **ran** his business **into the ground** by raising the prices of the menu and cutting back on staff.
2. The school district hired unqualified teachers at John Doe High School. Two years later, it was **run into the ground** because of the school's low test scores and high truancy rates.
3. Don't sell the hotel to him. He'll **run it into the ground** by not focusing on customer service.

Rule something out (rule out something)

Meaning:

If we **rule something out** we stop considering something as a possibility

Examples of use:
1. The idea was **ruled out** because the board of directors thought it would be too expensive.
2. Yesterday the group of investors **ruled** themselves **out** from the opportunity.
3. We don't want to take you to court, but we can't **rule** it **out** either.

Run up something

Meaning:

Run up something means to accumulate indebtedness

Examples of use:

1. Despite the man being innocent, he has **run up** a bill of $500,000 in lawyer's fees to prove to others that he isn't guilty.
2. Leslie was angry that her personal assistant had **run up** an extremely large amount of debt on the company credit cards.
3. A huge budget deficit has been **run up** by the federal government.

Ss

Saddled with debt

Meaning:

Saddled with debt means to be burdened with debt

Examples of use:
1. Tom couldn't afford to pay for his business loan. Now he's **saddled with debt** that he may not be able to pay off for years.
2. Before you pay for that big screen TV, ask yourself if you can afford it. If not, don't charge it on your credit card and be **saddled with** the **debt** for two years.
3. They can't afford to buy more machinery for the plant, since they are **saddled with debt** from the court case last year.

Safe bet

Meaning:

A proposition that is a **safe bet** doesn't have any risks attached.

Examples of use:
1. It's a **safe bet** that most men want to make money.

2. I'm sure that McDonald's will be successful for a long time. That's a pretty **safe bet**.
3. This stock is a **safe bet**. We'll get our investment back in no time.

Sail close to the wind

Meaning:

If you **sail close to the wind**, you take risks to do something, going close to the limit of what is allowed or acceptable.

Examples of use:
1. Microsoft came out with their version of an i-Pad. That **sailed close to the wind** since they weren't sure how many people would be interested in it.
2. Attempting to steal other rivals' customers is **sailing close to the wind**. If you are found out, you could be damaging the reputation of your company.
3. You don't want to go out on a date with your boss's daughter or else you will **sail close to the wind**. If the relationship doesn't work out, your job could be in jeopardy.

Same boat

Meaning:

If people are in the same difficult situation, they are in the **same boat**.

Examples of use:
1. The recession made everyone worry about losing their jobs. They were all **in the same boat.**
2. My husband and my best friend's husband are both on lengthy military duty. We miss them a lot. We're **in the same boat**.
3. Did you fail the exam too? We're both **in the same boat** and have to study hard for the next one.

Screw up

Meaning:

To mess up; to make a mistake is to **screw up**.

Examples of Use:
1. John gave the customer the wrong model. Now the customer has to come all the way back to get the right one. He really **screwed up**.
2. Christy was happy that she didn't **screw up** her interview. She got a job offer right away.
3. Please don't **screw up** this delivery. If you do, it will look bad for us.

Seed money

Meaning:

Seed money is money that is used to start a small business.

Examples of use:
1. Let's raise **seed money**, so we can open up a coffee shop.
2. Jackson doesn't have enough money to open his dream restaurant. He's needs more **seed money**.
3. I wonder if I can open up a small convenience store with this **seed money**.

Sell like hot cakes

Meaning:

If a product is selling very well, it is **selling like hot cakes**.

Examples of use:
1. Apple products **sell like hotcakes** especially to yuppies since they always want to buy the latest gadgets.
2. If you sell quality jeans at $20, they will **sell like hotcakes**.
3. Nike shoes are **selling like hotcakes** because of the two-for-one sale today.

Seller's market

Meaning:

A **seller's market** is a situation where there are more buyers of a product/service than sellers so sellers have and advantage

Examples of use:
1. The economy is doing well, so many people want to buy homes. It's a **seller's market**.
2. We should do well this year since it's a **seller's market**.
3. When is the **seller's market** going to start? This economy is killing us.

Sell something off

Meaning:

If you **sell something off** you sell a lot or all of something

Examples of use:
1. He **sold off** his clothing business to pay his debt.
2. We **sold off** most of last year's line to them.
3. The company reduced its debt by **selling off** its assets.

Set something up

Meaning:

When we **set something up** we establish a business, institute, or other kind of organization

Examples of use:
1. He has to **set up** a meeting for Ken and his upper management tomorrow morning.
2. I will get my secretary to **set up** all of the appointments for me next week.
3. We should **set up** a coffee shop here. There's no competition.

Set the wheels in motion

Meaning:

When you **set the wheels in motion**, you get something started.

Examples of use:
1. Andrew **set the wheels in motion** when negotiating last week.
2. We need to **set the wheels in motion** on this deal. Call our client and schedule a meeting with him tomorrow.
3. I will go to the bank to ask for a loan to **set the wheels in motion** to buy the equipment we need.

Sever Ties

Meaning:
If you **sever ties** you end a relationship

Examples of Use:
1. We had to **sever ties** with many of our suppliers because of late shipments.
2. Even though I left the company, I don't want to **sever ties** with my previous boss. He could help me down the line.
3. It's time to **sever ties**. I want to start my own company.

Shake something up

Meaning:

If you **shake something up** you reorganize a group or organization, not always in a gentle way

Examples of use:
1. The manager **shook up** the company by hiring two new people and firing two people.
2. The organization's entry into the music market **shook it up**.
3. The company has been **shaken up** due to major restructuring of management.

Ship came in

Meaning:

If your **ship has come in**, something very good has happened to you.

Examples of use:
1. It looks like my **ship has come in**. I got the job of my dreams!
2. I got the position that I've always wanted. My **ship came in** at the right moment.
3. I hope my **ship comes in**. I've had a tough time lately and need something positive to happen.

Shoot something down

Meaning:
To **shoot something down** means to deny something, such as a proposal or idea.

Examples of use:
1. I proposed a new idea to my boss but he didn't like it and promptly **shot** it **down**.
2. Before you **shoot** my proposal **down**, listen to the advantages of it first.
3. I still don't understand why my idea was **shot down**. It would have helped revive the company and bring back profits.

Shop floor

Meaning:

Shop floor refers to the part of an organization where the work is actually performed rather than just managed.

Examples of use:
1. We need to clean up the **shop floor**. There are too many auto parts lying around.
2. The office supply store has a lot of aisles on the **shop floor**. The customers are amazed at all the choices of products to buy.
3. Please bring the computer from the back onto the **shop floor**. The customer is interested in buying it.

Show someone the ropes

Meaning:

If you **show someone the ropes**, you explain to someone new how things work and how to do a job.

Examples of use:
1. The rookie just started working yesterday. We need to **show her the ropes**.

2. Why do we need to still **show** Bill the **ropes**? He's been working here for two months. He should know how to do his job by now.
3. Please **show me the ropes**. I've never played this game before.

Sign up for something

Meaning:

To record one's agreement to participate in something is to **sign up for something**

Examples of use:
1. He **signed up** to be on the basketball team in the fall.
2. He has been **signed up** as their new accounting manager.
3. Stores want their customers to **sign up** for their membership cards, so they will remain loyal to them.

Sit on the fence

Meaning:

If someone **sits on the fence**, they try not to support either side in a dispute.

Examples of use:

1. The criminal judge has to **sit on the fence** and let the jury decide if the accused is guilty or not.
2. Listen you both have valid points. I'm going to have to **sit on the fence** and let you guys talk it out.
3. Don't just **sit on the fence**. We need someone to tell us if this is the right product for the market.

Sky is the limit

Meaning:

When people say that the **sky is the limit**, they think that there are no limits to the possibilities something could have.

Examples of use:
1. The **sky is the limit**. You can get any job you want if you put your mind to it.
2. Now that you have started working at a law firm, the **sky is the limit** with regards to how many people you will get to meet and connections you will make.
3. Now that you have a teaching degree, the **sky is the limit** as to where you can teach.

Slash prices

Meaning:

Slash prices means to dramatically decrease prices

Examples of use:
1. Christmas is over and no one wants to buy any more computers. Let's **slash prices** and see if the customers bite.
2. After the car recall, Toyota **slashed prices** on some of its cars.
3. The clothing store will go out of business next month. Because of that, the store owner will **slash prices** to liquidate the merchandise.

Smooth sailing

Meaning:

If something is **smooth sailing**, then you can progress without difficulty. ('Plain sailing' is an also used.)

Examples of use:
1. This isn't going to be **smooth sailing**. We need to prepare a better deal.
2. My presentation was **smooth sailing**. It went a lot better than I expected.
3. I hope my business trip is **smooth sailing**. It might be difficult if our business partners don't agree with the deal we proposed.

Snap up

Meaning:

Snap up means to buy quickly, or in large quantities (this term implies that the product is very desirable, so that many people are buying it.

Examples of Use:

1. The customers on Monday **snapped up** all of the new iPhone 5 models. The customers who came the following day had to wait for two weeks for another shipment to come in.
2. If we sell our products too cheaply, customers will **snap** them **up** and we won't make much of a profit.
3. The Gap dropped their prices on blouses. All of the women came in and **snapped** them all **up** within two hours.

Squared away

Meaning:

Being prepared or ready for business or tasks at hand. Having the proper knowledge, skill and equipment to handle your assignment or station. 'He is a great addition to the squad; he is **squared away**.'

Examples of use:
1. Let's get these talks **squared away** so we can come to an agreement as fast as possible.

2. Don't worry we're **squared away**. Let's go and get this deal.
3. John is **squared away**. He has his notes ready and he is dressed sharply for the meeting.

Stand one's ground

Meaning:
If you **stand your ground**, it means that you will not change your opinion or position on an issue.

Examples of use:
1. Republicans and Democrats usually **stand their ground** on issues that reflect their party. They rarely change their opinions.
2. I will **stand my ground**. I made the right call on the deal.
3. Unions need to **stand their ground** when it overtime pay. They can't let management walk all over them.

Start from scratch

Meaning:

When you **start something from scratch**, you start at the very beginning.

Examples of use:

1. Mike's business went bankrupt. He'll have to **start from scratch** and start over after he changes the layout of his company.
2. The project was a failure. Let's **start from scratch** and try again later.
3. I don't like the way these look. Let's try again and **start from scratch**.

Start off on the wrong foot (Can also be used the opposite way-right foot)

Meaning:
To **start off on the wrong foot** means to start something in a negative way.

Examples of use:
1. I switched cable companies. They started off with more expensive prices than my last cable company. They really **started off on the wrong foot**.
2. When I met my boss for the first time, I didn't notice that I had a huge stain on my collar. That **started me off on the wrong foot**.
3. Please don't **start off on the wrong foot**. Study for your midterm now so you don't fall behind the other students in the class.

State of the art

Meaning:

If something is **state of the art**, it is the most up-to-date model incorporating the latest and best technology.

Examples of use:
1. Germany makes **start of the art** cars. Every country wants to copy their fine ingenuity.
2. Samsung and Apple continue to compete with each other in ways to make the next **state of the art** smart phone.
3. There was a time when having a video camera in a digital camera was a **state of the art** idea. Now every camera has that feature.

Stay on your toes

Meaning:

If you **stay on your toes** you pay attention and stay aware

Examples of use:

1. The manager's boss will be making a visit today. Make sure you **stay on your toes**.
2. Amy, parents will be observing your classroom as you teach next week. Please **stay on your toes**.
3. In order to be a great sales person, you need to **stay on your toes** and focus on your customer at all times.

Step down from something

Meaning:

If you **step down from something** you resign from a job or responsibility

Examples of use:
1. Mark is **stepping down** as the manager after four strong years.
2. Why will you **step down** from such a high position? You could get a higher retirement bonus in a few years.
3. No one knows who will replace the President when he **steps down** in November.

Stick To Your Guns

Meaning:

If you **stick to your guns**, you keep your position even though people attack or criticize you.

Examples of use:
1. The NRA insists on gun rights for individuals including assault weapons. They literally **stick to their guns** on that issue.

2. Despite nearly everyone disagreeing with Chandler, he is **sticking to his guns** and going to leave his job.
3. Kimberly is **sticking to her guns**. She insists that creating a new product needs to be a top priority despite others thinking that it will cost the company too much money.

Sticking point

Meaning:

A **sticking point** is a controversial issue that blocks progress in negotiations, etc., where compromise is unlikely or impossible.

Examples of use:
1. Funding a new stadium is a **sticking point** between the city and the team. The team won't stay in the city unless it happens and the city doesn't want taxpayers to pay for a new stadium.
2. Don't let money be a **sticking point** in the negotiations. We want to work together on this project and I'm sure we can come to a compromise.
3. I want to move premises to Jamison Street, but unless the price is reduced, it will be a **sticking point** to us buying it.

Stock up on something

Meaning:
Stock up on something is to amass so as to keep for future use or sale or for a particular occasion or use

Examples of use:
1. After the earthquake, families in the neighborhood **stocked up on** water and flashlights.
2. We need to **stock up on** this model before Black Monday.
3. Did you **stock up** enough for the January sales?

Stuck in a rut

Meaning:

If you are unable to move forward in a job, career, or a life moment you are **stuck in a rut**

Examples of Use:
1. We have been making the same amount of profit for the last year and we haven't been able to come up with something new. I think we're **stuck in a rut**.
2. I don't want to be **stuck in a rut** any more. I've been bored with this job for months and I think it's time to move on.
3. Mr. Anderson, I've been stuck in the same position for the last six years. How am I going to be able to get out of this **rut** that I'm **stuck in**?

Swim against the tide

Meaning:

If you **swim against the tide**, you try to do
something that is very difficult because there is a lot
of opposition to you. ('Go against the tide' is an
alternative form.)

Examples of use:
1. Soobin was **swimming against the tide** to keep
her relationship with Steve going. None of her
family supported her.
2. The area in downtown is very dangerous but
Jackie decided to **swim against the tide** and open up
her manicure shop there anyway.
3. This invention will change the world but no one is
supporting me. I feel like I'm **swimming against the
tide**.

Tt

Tackle an issue

Meaning:

If you **tackle an issue** or problem, you resolve or deal with it.

Examples of use:
1. You **tackled this issue** well I think you deserve a promotion.
2. We're losing customers fast. How are we going to **tackle this issue**?
3. Frank has been consistently disrespectful to his coworkers this week. Let's find a way to **tackle this issue**.

Take a hit

Meaning:

To be hurt financially is to **take a hit**

Examples of use:
1. The tsunami caused the tourism industry to **take a hit** in Phuket. It took a while for the city to recover financially.
2. The defective airbags caused the auto company to **take a hit** in sales for six months.

3. E-books caused regular bookstore sales to **take a hit** causing some of their businesses to close down.

Take a pay cut

Meaning:

To **take a pay cut** is to accept a decrease in one's salary

Examples of use:
1. In order to keep the coworker I'm very close to at our company, I was willing to **take a pay cut** so he wouldn't lose his job.
2. Would you be willing to **take a pay cut** since our company isn't doing well? Once we start making more money, I'll give you a solid raise.
3. Ben was forced to **take a pay cut** since his company was struggling to make a profit.

Take (something) at face value

Meaning:

To take something exactly as it was said is to **take something at face value**

Examples of use:

1. I **took** my friend's comment at **face value**. He usually tells me the truth.
2. Please **take** what I said at **face value**. I'm being serious.
3. It's hard to **take** Mary's remarks at **face value**. She likes to joke around a lot and it's hard to tell when she is being serious.

Take off

Meaning:

Take off means to start succeeding really well.

Examples of use:
1. It took 20 years, but the business finally **took off**.
2. Computer sales have really **taken off** after that amazing commercial.
3. Our restaurant has been a bit disappointing. Sales haven't **taken off** yet.

Take the floor

Meaning:

Formally addressing a group of people in a form of a speech or presentation is to **take the floor**

Examples of Use:

1. The chairman will **take the floor** for a few moments before the staff party officially begins.
2. Congressman Adams **took the floor** in an attempt to argue against the opposition.
3. My sister is really nervous. She has to **take the floor** for 30 minutes in a meeting on Friday.

Take someone down a peg

Meaning:

If someone is **taken down a peg** (or taken down a peg or two), they lose status in the eyes of others because of something they have done wrong or badly.

Examples of use:
1. The boss **took** Ken **down a peg** because he came to work drunk. Most people have lost respect for him.
2. Belinda's poor presentation caused her to be **taken down a peg** by her boss.
3. We should **take** him **down a peg** because all he does is complain at work.

Take someone under your wing

Meaning:

If you **take someone under your wing**, you look after them while they are learning something.

Examples of use:
1. Mr. Smith **took** the new employee **under his wing** to help him get adjusted to the new position.
2. The veteran salesman **took** the new guy **under his wing** to help him become more skilled.
3. Can you please **take** this new cashier **under your wing**? We need to help her get used to handling cash every day.

Take your eye off the ball

Meaning:

If someone **takes their eye off the ball**, they don't concentrate on something important that they should be looking at.

Examples of use:
1. The manager **took his eye off the ball** and let the shoplifter take off with some phone accessories without paying.
2. Please **don't take your eye off the ball**. I know your vacation starts tomorrow but we need you to focus a lot more on your work.
3. The coach told the batter not to **take his eye off the ball** since he tended to strike out a lot during the season.

Take something over

Meaning:

To **take something over** is to get into one's possession by force, skill, or artifice

Examples of use:

1. They **took over** the struggling airline, which was losing profits for the past two years and turned it around.
2. The government **will take** the department of transportation **over** as part of its nationalization plan.
3. Our business is probably going to be **taken over** by our rival, since we don't know what we're doing.

Talk shop

Meaning:

If you **talk shop**, you talk about work matters, especially if you do this outside work.

Examples of use:
1. Please stop **talking shop** over dinner. I don't want to think about work anymore.

2. The C.E.O. **talked shop** with his employees over a drink to discuss possible pay increases and dismissals of poor employees.
3. The English teachers got together at a coffee shop to **talk shop** and come up with ideas on how to teach their students better.

Talk someone into doing something

Meaning:
To **talk someone into something** means to convince someone to do something.

Examples of use:
1. He didn't want to go to the musical, but I **talked** him **into going**.
2. You can't **talk** me **into** transferring departments. I'm not a marketer.
3. I would never **talk** someone **into** quitting. It's not the right thing to do.

Test market a product

Meaning:

Test market a product is to research whether or not a product will be successful by selling it in a particular market or by choosing people to use the product for a specified period of time and receiving comments from them

Examples of use:
1. Starbucks **test markets** their hot drinks. As soon as they find out that people like them, they offer them during the Christmas season.
2. Let's ask Joe to **test market** our product and see what he thinks about it.
3. Coca Cola **test marketed** their new formula called "New Coke" in the 1980s. It failed miserably so they brought the original formula back.

Test the waters

Meaning:

If you **test the waters**, or **test the water**, you experiment to see how successful or acceptable something is before implementing it.

Examples of use:
1. Before we sell this machine, let's **test the waters** and see how well it works.
2. The principal imposed new rules at the school. He **tested the waters** for a week and checked how the students reacted to the changes.
3. I love my new position, but lately we've been working really late. I want to **test the waters** and ask if this is normal.

The ball's in your court

Meaning:

If somebody says **the ball's in your court** to you, they mean that it's up to you to decide or take the next step.

Examples of use:
1. Are you going to accept my offer or not? **The ball is in your court**.
2. I left a message on this guy's machine. Now it's up to him to let me know if we're going to have the meeting on Friday. The **ball is in his court**.
3. I put the **ball in your court**. Are you going to accept our deal?

Think outside the box

Meaning:

If you think **outside the box**, you think in an imaginative and creative way.

Examples of use:
1. You all need to **think outside the box**. If we're going to beat our rival, we cannot come up with ideas like this.

2. The head designer told her team to **think outside the box** and use their imagination more.
3. I want you to blow me away with an idea I've never seen before. **Think outside the box** and come up with a brand new formula.

Through the ceiling

Meaning:

If prices go **through the ceiling**, they rise very quickly.

Examples of use:
1. Cost of raw materials have gone **through the ceiling**. We have to raise our prices.
2. Going to Disneyland is expensive for families. The cost of admission has gone **through the ceiling** over the past 10 years. It's $92 for a one-day pass to Disneyland for adults.
3. Because the cost of flight tickets for first class went **through the ceiling**, Mr. Jamison decided to buy a business class ticket instead.

Through the floor

Meaning:

If prices go, or fall, **through the floor**, they fall very quickly.

1. The decrease in demand for old cell phones caused the prices to go **through the floor**.
2. The cars found to have defective airbags caused the prices to go **through the floor**.
3. The prices of the furniture in that store have gone **through the floor** since the scandal.

Throw cold water over (an idea or plan)

Meaning:

If you **throw cold water over something** you present reasons why something will not work; to discourage

Examples of Use:
1. Pat suggested expanding business in China but her boss **threw cold water** over the idea and told her to just focus on the domestic market.
2. Our company considered hiring a rookie to oversee the accounting department. However, all of the employees **threw cold water** over the idea.
3. The boss wanted to hire a new C.F.O. unfortunately, the owner **threw cold water** over the plan.

Throw in the towel

Meaning:
To quit is **throw in the towel**

Examples of use:
1. I'm **throwing in the towel** and going to find another company to work for.
2. Don't **throw in the towel**. He's an idiot, but he retires next year.
3. I wanted to **throw in the towel**, but I also wanted the promotion.

Throw money at (something)

Meaning:

To try to solve a problem by spending money on it is to **throw money at something**

Examples of use:
1. If you want a relationship with your daughter, don't just **throw money at** her and try to buy her love.
2. The president is willing to **throw** a lot of **money at** the factory problem.
3. If the marketing department is struggling, don't just **throw money at** them change their strategy as well.

Throw the book at someone

Meaning:

If you **throw the book at someone**, you punish them as severely as possible.

Examples of use:
1. The jury **threw the book at** the alleged criminal after he was found guilty of drunk driving for the third time in two years.
2. I hope the boss won't **throw the book** at me for being late again. I don't want to have a pay cut.
3. They will **throw the book** at you this time. That's the third contract you've lost.

Tight ship

Meaning:

If you run a **tight ship**, you control something strictly and don't allow people much freedom of action.

Examples of use:
1. My mother **runs a tight ship**. My brothers and sisters can't get away with anything.
2. Don't bother coming to work without wearing a suit. We **run a tight ship** here.
3. The boss **ran a tight ship** at the company. We could only get 30-minute lunches and no breaks.

Tight Spot

Meaning:

A **tight spot** is a difficult situation

Examples of use:
1. The computer company has been in a **tight spot** since the shortage of semiconductors.
2. I'm in a **tight spot**. If I miss a day of work, my boss will get angry because it's the busy season.
3. Carrie got into a **tight spot** this morning. Her car stalled on the fast lane of the freeway during rush hour.

Tip of the iceberg

Meaning:

The tip of the iceberg is the part of a problem that can be seen, with far more serious problems lying underneath.

Examples of use:
1. Our sales are down this month. But that's just the **tip of the iceberg** if we don't make better products soon.

2. Jack misusing the company credit card was just the **tip of the iceberg**. Mary saw him stealing merchandise as well.

3. Martin seems to be lacking focus at work. He's been late for the third day in a row. This could be the **tip of the iceberg** to a much bigger problem.

Tread water

Meaning:

If someone is **treading water**, they are making no progress.

Examples of use:

1. She feels like she's just **treading water** in university. She can't seem to get up to a 3.0 on her grade point average even with all the studying she has been doing.

2. Pamela has been stuck in the same position for the last five years, and there's no end in sight. She feels like she's just **treading water** and going nowhere.

3. It's as if I'm **treading water** with all this paperwork on my desk that seems to never go away.

Turn around one's business

Meaning:

To **turn around one's business** is to make a business profitable again; To go from not making any profits to being profitable again

Examples of use:
1. The telecom company was able to **turn around its business** by developing a popular new line of services.
2. McDonald's **turned around their business** by lowering the price of their Big Macs.
3. The amusement park had a couple of unfortunate accidents. After a change of ownership, new rides, and a new image, the park was able to **turn around their business**.

Turn something out

Meaning:
To produce something means to **turn something out**

Examples of use:
1. The factory **turns out** thousands of dolls every day.
2. 890 workers are making cell phones, **turning out** thousands of units each day.
3. My grandma has a baker's touch. She keeps **turning out** cookies and pastries every week.

Turn something over to somebody

Meaning:

If you **turn something over to somebody** you put someone in control of something

Examples of use:
1. The team will **turn over** many of its functions to human resources.
2. The boss said that he would **turn** his business **over** to his son once he passed away.
3. The criminal was **turned over** to the FBI by the local police department.

Turn the tables

Meaning:

If circumstances change completely, giving an advantage to those who seemed to be losing, the **tables are turned**.

Examples of use:
1. They scored 10 points in the fourth quarter to take the lead with two minutes remaining in the game. The **tables had been turned** on opposing team.
2. During the debate, Mr. Johnson was losing to Mr. Garcia until **the tables were turned** and Johnson stumbled over a question that he couldn't answer.
3. Everyone thought that the company didn't have enough money to hire another employee until Mr.

Adams **turned the tables** by offering to give up 10% of his salary to hire someone.

Uu

Under the table

Meaning:

Bribes or illegal payments are often described as money **under the table**. It can also be used in less serious situations.

Examples of use:
1. I got these shoes from the black market. Pay me **under the table** and then we'll be even.
2. The man taught private English lessons to his students, but didn't want to pay taxes for it so he decided to get paid **under the table**.
3. Just pay me **under the table.** We don't need to keep a record of this.

Under your belt

Meaning:

If you have something **under your belt**, you have already achieved or experienced it and it will probably be of benefit to you in the future.

Examples of use:

1. Now that I have work as a cashier **under my belt**, I can now concentrate on becoming a customer service manager.
2. I'm so happy I got a Master's degree. Now that I have that **under my belt**, I can get a job in counseling.
3. She has three years **under her belt** as an accountant. She's working her way up to be the C.F.O.

Uphill Battle

Meaning:

A difficult fight is an **uphill battle**

Examples of Use:
1. We would like to acquire the property on Smith Street. However, if someone makes a better offer, we might not get it. We could be facing an **uphill battle**.
2. Kelly wants to be promoted, but George has more experience than her. It could be an **uphill battle**.
3. You need to come across **uphill battles** if you want to grow in your company. It will make you stronger.

Up in the air

Meaning:

If a matter is **up in the air**, no decision has been made and there is uncertainty about it.

Examples of use:
1. Since it might rain tomorrow, our plans to watch a baseball game tomorrow are **up in the air**.
2. Due to our buyer in Japan being on vacation, our business trip is **up in the air**.
3. Our decision to close the store in downtown is **up in the air** since we can't all agree if that's the right call or not.

Up to speed

Meaning:

If you bring someone **up to speed**, you update them on something.

Examples of use:
1. Jack, I've been gone for two weeks on business. Get me **up to speed** on what's been happening at the office.
2. The secretary got the president **up to speed** on the messages he missed while being in a two-hour conference call.
3. The teacher got Kristi's parents **up to speed** on her progress, and they were very happy to hear that Kristi improved a lot since last quarter.

Upper hand

Meaning:

If you have the **upper hand**, you have the advantage.

Examples of use:
1. He has more money and can put a larger offer on that house. He has the **upper hand**.
2. I'm confident that we have the **upper hand** on this one.
3. Two candidates are in the final round to get the job. Kelly has the **upper hand** because she has a lot more experience compared to Brad who just started working last year.

Vv

Virgin territory

If something is **virgin territory**, it hasn't been explored before.

Examples of use:
1. I've never worked in sales before. This is **virgin territory** for me.
2. We've been really successful in the hardware industry, but software is **virgin territory** for us.
3. Expanding our business is a bit scary, since we've never done it before. Consider this **virgin territory** for our company.

Ww

Water Under the Bridge

Meaning:

When something has happened but can't change its
water under the bridge

Examples of Use:
1. We lost the deal, but we will just have to consider
it **water under the bridge**, and move on to the next
opportunity.
2. We need to put our differences aside and consider
them **water under the bridge**. We can both benefit
from this deal.
3. I'm sorry I was so harsh on you Mr. Thomas.
Please consider it **water under the bridge**, so that
we can start over.

War of words

Meaning:

A **war of words** is a bitter argument between people
or organizations, etc.

Examples of use:

1. Sara and Tom haven't been able to agree on how to finish the work that's left. They're now having a **war of words**.
2. Two competing companies are having a **war of words** with each other. One company copied the other company's logo and used it for their benefit.
3. Why are we having this **word of words**? We need to decide which direction the company needs to go in.

Well-oiled machine

Meaning:

Something that functions very well is a **well-oiled machine**.

Examples of use:
1. My car is a **well-oiled machine**. It hasn't had any major malfunctions since I bought it four years ago.
2. I wish our copy machine was a **well-oiled machine**. It constantly gets paper jams.
3. Thanks for keeping the computer free of viruses. Because you keep updating the software, it continues to be a **well-oiled machine**.

Wheels fall off

Meaning:

When the **wheels fall off** something, it goes wrong or fails. ('Wheels come off' is an alternative.)

Examples of use:
1. The bad proposal caused the **wheels** to **fall off** because the customer wanted to drop the deal.
2. The **wheels have fallen off** this deal. We need to work out why.
3. After being a good employee for three years, all the **wheels** started **falling off** when he got divorced.

Whole new ball game

Meaning:

If something's a **whole new ball game**, it is completely new or different.

Examples of use:
1. This is a **whole new ball game**. I'm looking forward to the challenges.
2. Our company usually focuses on the domestic market. Next year, it will be a **whole new ball game** as we expand internationally.
3. We had a very lazy accountant who barely got half of his work done on a daily basis. We hired Mr. Reynolds who has a reputation of being productive and hardworking. When he starts work, it'll be a **whole new ball game** in the office.

Word of mouth

Meaning:

If something becomes known by **word of mouth**, it is because people are talking about it, not through publicity, etc.

Examples of use:
1. Johnson Sandwiches doesn't have enough money to advertise its product. It's hoping that people will enjoy their food causing **word of mouth** to spread.
2. Lisa heard Anderson Department Store had great deals through **word of mouth**. She is glad she listened to her friends. She got three blouses at a fantastic price.
3. Rick's reputation jumped after six months. Through **word of mouth**, a lot of new clients contacted him.

Work the system

Meaning:

If people **work the system**, they exploit the state or similar setup to their advantage.

Examples of use:

1. Some argue that illegal immigrants **work the system** so that they can get welfare and not go to work.
2. Sweatshops are known for **working the system** as they pay their employees low wages and then sell their clothing for three or four times the amount.
3. Sadly, some teachers **work the system** by working hard until they get tenure. Then they coast through the rest of their career.

Worth a shot

Meaning:

If something is **worth a shot**, it is worth trying as there is some chance of success.

Examples of use:
1. It's **worth a shot.** We just might get the contract if we're lucky.
2. Many people believe that despite the low odds, it's **worth a shot** at buying a lottery ticket. If you win, you win big.
3. I'm not sure if I'll get the job, but since I have some experience and a Master's degree, I think it's **worth a shot** at applying for it.

Write Something Off

Meaning:

To **write something off** is to absorb a debt or loss in accounting

Examples of use:
1. The company was forced to **write off** about $2 million in debt.
2. Cassie was sure that she wouldn't get her loan back from Steve so she just **wrote** it **off**.
3. After 10 years, her college debt was **written off**.

Written in stone

Meaning:

If something is **written in stone**, it is permanent and cannot be changed.

Examples of use:
1. Once the new driving laws get **written in stone**, you'll have to be really careful driving. Speeding tickets will be really expensive.
2. This deal is **written in stone**. I promise we will deliver.
3. Before you sign the contract, just remember one thing. Once it's signed, it will be **written in stone** and you can't go back on your word.

Yy

Yes-man

Meaning:

Someone who always agrees with people in authority is a **yes-man**.

Examples of use:
1. Stewart is such a **yes-man**. He does everything the boss says.
2. Don't be a **yes-man**. Be honest and tell me if you agree with this proposal or not.
3. We don't want **yes-men** in this department. We encourage forward thinkers.

You can't make an omelet without breaking eggs

Meaning:

You can't make an omelet without breaking eggs means that in order to achieve something or make progress, there are often losers in the process.

Examples of use:
1. Not everyone will be happy but **you can't make an omelet without breaking some eggs**.

2. It will be hard for us to **make an omelet without breaking eggs**. Someone is bound to lose their job as we go through restructuring.

3. We might have to take a pay cut to get this company back into the black. Unfortunately, we **can't make an omelet without breaking a few eggs**.

About the authors

Liam Lusk was born in Paisley, Scotland and moved to England at the age of 8 where he spent his childhood. His involvement in the business world began over 20 years ago in London. He started his professional career in the theatre industry at the world famous London Palladium theatre. After moving to Korea in 2001, he became involved in the presentation and English communication coaching sector. He has been an active person on the internet since 2006 having run both successful blogs and businesses. He now spends his time lecturing on presentation skills, social media and running his consulting company. He lives with his wife and daughter in Seoul, Korea.

Scott Worden is originally from Monterey Park, California. He has lived in Seoul, South Korea since September 2003. Having taught children of various backgrounds including: bi-polar, autistic, emotionally disturbed, and children with Asperger's Syndrome he has also taught ESL to elementary and middle school students. He is currently an ESL instructor at Wall Street English in Seoul. The best part of his job is being able to travel once or twice a year which has allowed him to travel to over 10 countries.

Contact page

Liam Lusk

Twitter: https://twitter.com/liamlusk

Facebook: https://www.facebook.com/liamslusk

YouTube: http://www.youtube.com/liamkorea

Blog: http://www.liamlusk.com/

Author Page on Amazon:

http://www.amazon.com/Liam-Lusk/e/B0095TN6KS/

Scott Worden

Twitter: https://twitter.com/LASeoulGuy

Blog: http://laseoulguy.com/

Author Page on Amazon:

http://www.amazon.com/Scott-Worden/e/B00A13YK8O/

 Another English learning book by

Liam Lusk and Scott Worden

Made in the USA
Lexington, KY
01 March 2018